CHEESE MAGIC

SEASONAL RECIPES,
PLATES, AND PAIRINGS

Running Press
Hachette Book Group
1290 Avenue of the Americas, New York, NY 10104
www.runningpress.com
@Running_Press

First Edition: September 2025

Published by Running Press, an imprint of Hachette Book Group, Inc. The Running Press name and logo are trademarks of Hachette Book Group, Inc.

The Hachette Speakers Bureau provides a wide range of authors for speaking events. To find out more, go to www.hachettespeakersbureau.com or email HachetteSpeakers@hbgusa.com.

Running Press books may be purchased in bulk for business, educational, or promotional use. For more information, please contact your local bookseller or the Hachette Book Group Special Markets Department at Special.Markets@hbgusa.com.

The publisher is not responsible for websites (or their content) that are not owned by the publisher.

Print book cover and interior design by Jen Quinn of Indelible Editions

Produced by Indelible Editions

INDELIBLE
EDITIONS

Library of Congress Control Number: 2024057612

ISBNs: 978-0-7624-8963-3 (hardcover), 979-8-89414-191-6 (ebook)

Printed in China

TLF

10 9 8 7 6 5 4 3 2 1

CHEESE MAGIC

SEASONAL RECIPES, PLATES, AND PAIRINGS

ERIKA KUBICK

AUTHOR OF *CHEESE SEX DEATH*

WITH ILLUSTRATIONS BY
DEVIN FORST

Running Press
PHILADELPHIA

CONTENTS

Lavender Goat Cheese Truffles, page 94

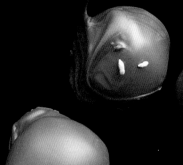

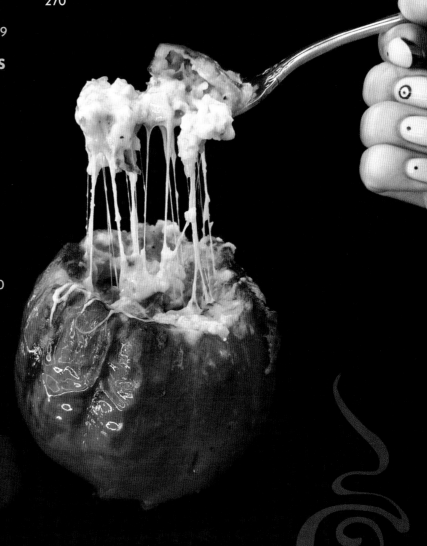

Cheese-Stuffed Pumpkin , page 230

INTRODUCTION

Cheese is magic. While inanimate to the naked eye, cheese is alive with microbes breathing, breeding, and conjuring flavors and textures out of coagulated milk. That milk is itself a manifestation of the natural world: flora, sun-powered and born of the soil, consumed by fauna, absorbed, and transmuted into the liquid gold that flows back out at the touch of the human hand.

Due to this shape-shifting nature, there is a long-standing relationship between witchcraft and cheesemaking. Crafting artisanal cheese is a tricky business even for experts, and that's partly how it differs from industrial cheesemaking: the potential for misfortune. Milk can sour or fail to coagulate, rinds can dry out and form cracks, and the gases within can build up and cause cheese to literally explode.

Before our ancestors understood microbial activity, they often attributed this uncertainty to witchcraft, accusing dairymaids of casting an evil eye over neighboring cows that had dried up or enchanting their own yields into rich butters and well-set cheeses. While these allegations were often rooted in misogyny, cheesemaking is not unlike spellcasting. It involves practice, faith, and a little bit of magic. Even to this day, cheesemakers consider it unlucky to enter the make room or aging cellars in a sour mood, lest these dark energies transfer onto the cheeses.

Cheese also has an enchanting effect on us. In her 1970 tome The Complete Book of Magic and Witchcraft, Kathryn Paulsen declared, "You may fascinate a woman by giving her a piece of cheese." She has a point: cheese has the physical power to charm our reward centers into releasing dopamine and eliciting sensations of pleasure.

In addition to her magical abilities, cheese possesses a goddess-like quality. The milk comes from female ruminants that were historically milked by dairymaids who possessed the secret knowledge of cheesemaking, much like mystics. Even in the modern era, the artisanal cheese movement has been largely led by women. I like to honor this divine connection by using she/her pronouns when referring to cheese. It's mostly cheeky, but also a reference to the women who've played such a vital role in the ancient lineage of cheesemaking: from the dairymaids to the Sumerian goddess Inanna, who demanded butter and cheese offerings from her worshippers.

Both cheese and magical rituals have been enjoyed and practiced by our ancestors for thousands of years. Engaging in both gifts us the opportunity to connect to those who came before, as well as their traditions. Cheese

Magic honors this ancient history by harnessing the powers of the natural world, from the cheese to the magical herbs and ingredients with which she's paired. You don't have to identify as a witch or even practice magic to enjoy the recipes and pairings detailed within these pages. Regardless of your level of skill or interest, these rituals will have the enchanting effect of grounding you in the present and connecting you to the seasons that inspired them.

At its core, magic is the power to create change through mysterious forces. While many of our ancestor's superstitions have been debunked, our scientific knowledge has not lessened cheese's mystique. From turning a few wedges and accompaniments into a beautiful platter to transforming stale bread into brûléed chèvre-crowned French toast, these recipes harness the magic of cheese. While both cheese and magic seem intimidating to novice practitioners, neither requires esoteric knowledge or specialty tools. All they ask of you is your presence and intention. You need only to begin and practice. The guiding principles in this book will help you along the way.

What is a cheese plate if not an altar?

The Wheel of the Year

This book is organized by the eight sabbats that form the Wheel of the Year, a series of festivals that mark the solstices, equinoxes, and cross-quarter festivals in between. These touchpoints make up our journey around the sun, each an equidistant spoke on the ever-turning wheel.

It's important to note that the Wheel of the Year is a modern invention, first mentioned in Jacob Grimm's 1835 book *Deutsche Mythologie* and further developed by Wiccan and neo-pagans throughout the twentieth century. While mostly derived from Celtic mythology with Germanic and Norse influences, there are celebrations around the world that align with the spokes on the wheel.

Over the course of history, these touchpoints were celebrated with rituals, revelry, and, most importantly, feasting. By following this calendar, you can channel the energies of the changing seasons into your practice. Each section in this book features eight recipes, three cheese plates, and two pairings—thirteen opportunities to help anchor yourself in relation to your environment, even as climate change is drastically impacting the way we experience the seasons. If you don't live in a place with distinct seasons, there are still cycles within the self: a time to plant seeds, a time to grow, a time to harvest, and a time for rest and release. No matter where you live, the annual journey of the sun connects us all to the magic of each day.

On Appropriation

The world of spirituality is rife with appropriation, especially from the First Nations of the Americas. The founders of Wicca, the nature-based religion practiced by many modern witches, cherry-picked customs from cultures around the world, then flattened and repackaged them for Western consumption. I've also included mythologies and history from around the world, not to extract but rather to highlight the root of many modern-day customs. For example, most of our Christmas traditions are derived from the Germanic and Nordic customs of Yule, which marks the winter solstice.

We must be mindful of where these rituals originate and to what extent they are open to us. For example, it has become quite popular in recent years to burn white sage bundles and palo santo, a practice known as smudging. However, the overharvesting of these sacred medicines is not only damaging the earth but also stealing a custom from a closed culture, meaning one that has not expressly consented to outsiders' use of their customs. By contrast, because incense has been used historically around the world, it is open. While we are all connected by the same organic lineage and can draw inspiration from the old ways, we must be mindful of our sources. This book draws inspiration primarily from the Paganism of northern Europe because that's my heritage. If that does not resonate with you, look into the customs of your own lineage. Adapting a ritual to better match those practiced by your own ancestors will yield the most potent magical results.

Cheese 101

The following is a primer with everything you need to know in order to get the most out of *Cheese Magic*.

THE RULES OF CHEESE MAGIC

1. Buy cheese often: Once a wheel is cut, cheese starts to deteriorate. The smaller the piece, the quicker she loses her flavor. The key to eating cheese at her peak is to buy only as much as you can eat in a few days, then buy more.

2. Serve cheese at room temperature: Refrigeration dulls the flavor and makes the texture more brittle. Always let soft cheeses sit out for at least twenty minutes and firm cheeses for forty. This rule applies to cooking with cheese too. A cold cheese doesn't melt evenly and can even separate, resulting in an oily, clumpy mess.

3. Cut that cheese correctly: More surface area means more flavor on your tongue. Instead of cubing cheese, slice her thinly to maintain the shape of the wedge. When cutting soft cheeses like Brie, aim for an equal rind ratio by slicing wheels like a pie and wedges lengthwise.

4. Respect the rind: Unless they're coated in wax, cloth, or plastic, all rinds are edible. Some of them are delicious and can add all sorts of flavors and textures to your cheese experience. Try them all at least once. If you don't like it, then don't eat it again! That's okay too.

5. Don't store cheese in plastic: Cheese is alive and needs oxygen to breathe. Wrapping her in plastic suffocates her and traps moisture, which can ruin the flavor and even make the texture slimy. I recommend professional cheese paper, or wrapping her tightly in parchment or waxed paper, then storing in a loose resealable bag or tub. This allows for airflow while maintaining proper humidity levels.

6. Shred your cheese fresh off the block: Freshly grated cheese has a better flavor and smoother texture than pre-shredded cheese, which often has preservatives and de-clumping agents that make the consistency rubbery when melted.

7. Use one knife per cheese: The unique, complex flavors of each cheese are special and deserve their moment in the spotlight. Avoid cross-contamination by using a different knife for each cheese and accoutrement.

8. Taste cheese right: Enjoying a good cheese is a ritual and a full sensory experience. First, take in her beauty. Then touch her and observe the texture. Next, take a big whiff and concentrate on her aromas. Finally, take a bite, letting the flavors wash across your palate. Refrain from playing with pairings until you've tried the cheese by herself. When tasting multiple cheeses, always begin with the mildest one, and end with the strongest flavor.

TYPES OF CHEESE

Cheese takes thousands of forms, and while it's nearly impossible to properly categorize this bounty, I like to break it down into five simple types: fresh, bloomy, washed, firm, and blue.

Cheese takes a thousand forms.

1. Fresh cheeses are unaged, high-moisture, and very perishable. Aside from brined feta, which has an impressive months-long shelf life, I recommend eating fresh cheeses within a week of breaking the seal. Types include spreadable, like fresh chèvre; pasta filata, like mozzarella; or pressed, like paneer.

2. Bloomy cheeses are voluptuous and creamy, with delicate rinds that range from soft and downy to thin and wrinkly. They're sensitive to the touch and prone to mishandling, so be careful where you source them. If they spend too much time sitting in their plastic wrap, they might taste ammoniated. Types include classic French Brie, Italian robiola, and wrinkly, Geotrichum rinds, like Chabichou.

3. Washed-rind cheeses are bathed in brines or alcohol to encourage the growth of bacteria, resulting in sticky, reddish rinds, golden pastes, and a pungency that can range from fresh onions to stinky feet. Their bark is often bigger than their bite, with tasting notes such as caramelized onions, beef broth, and baked quiche. Types include spoonable Époisses, pudgy Taleggio, and Alpine styles like Gruyère.

4. Firm cheeses are the broadest category, featuring sturdy wheels with hardy, protective rinds that form after months or even years of aging. Mature and deeply complex, they're some of the most expensive due to the masterful craftsmanship and time it takes to create them, but they're so worth it. Types include Dutch Gouda, block cheddars, Manchego, and grana styles like Parmigiano Reggiano.

5. Blue cheeses are some of the most polarizing, characterized by their salinity and pockets and streaks of blue mold. They can range from soft enough to spoon to hard enough to grate. Some are quite mild and gentle, while others carry a tongue-titillating burn. Avoid pre-crumbled cheeses, which tend to have an off-putting metallic taste that overpowers the natural flavor. Types include Stilton, Roquefort, and Gorgonzola.

MILK TYPES

1. Cow's milk cheeses range from light cream to golden yellow, due to the beta-carotene in grass, which travels through the cow's bloodstream into the milk. Cow's milk creates buttery, smooth textures with fruity, earthy, and creamy flavors.

2. Sheep's milk cheeses are pale ivory with unctuous, rich flavors, due to the higher ratio of fats and protein. The flavors are often nutty and sweet with gentle woolly notes from the lanolin oil on the sheep's skin.

3. Goat's milk cheeses are bright white because goats can convert the beta-carotene in grass. The texture is often fragile and crumbly, due to the smaller fats and proteins and the way they clump together. Flavors are tangy, herbaceous, clean, and bright.

4. Buffalo's milk cheeses have twice the fat and half the cholesterol of cow's milk cheeses. While water buffalo are rather uncommon in the US and northern Europe, they're popular dairy animals throughout the world, including parts of southern Asia, northern Africa, along the Mediterranean, and Latin America. Their milk is bright white with a rich, luscious texture and a clean, creamy flavor that has a subtle mossy note.

Serving Size

For an appetizer:
2 to 3 ounces (55 to 85 grams) total cheese per person

For the main course:
4 to 6 ounces (115 to 170 grams) total cheese per person

If you're melting the cheese, then you can double the portion.
For whatever reason, we can take in a lot more cheese
when she's liquefied.

Cutting the Cheese

Let the shape of the cheese tell you
how she wants to be cut.

1

LOGS
Slice into coins.

2

RECTANGLES
Thinly slice
them lengthwise.

3

SMALL-FORMAT WHEELS
Cut like a pie.

4

WEDGES

Cut into triangles.

5

SQUARE BLOCKS
Slice into ½-inch-thick
slabs. Cut in half vertically,
then horizontally. Cut on
diagonal both ways for
eight triangular portions.

6

CRUMBLY CHEESES
When it comes to certain
cheeses, you'll never get
a clean cut no matter how
hard you try. Biscuity
blues and crunchy aged
cheeses just want to
crumble, so let them.
Simply insert the tip of
a knife straight into the
wedge and gently
wiggle to release
snackable chunks.

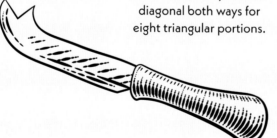

ON RAW MILK

Cheeses made with raw milk are some of the most enchanting, but they're difficult to create. Cheesemakers must put in a lot of extra work to prevent pathogens at every stage of the process. Pasteurization, which is the act of heating milk to kill off bacteria, makes this easier because it destroys pathogens. However, it also wipes away the magical microbes that create complex flavors and textures unique to the individual environments where these cheeses are made. Cheesemakers can always purchase molds and yeasts from labs to reintroduce that flavor, and there are tons of delicious pasteurized cheeses out there. In my opinion, nothing quite compares to the mystique of a raw milk cheese. In the United States, the Food and Drug Administration requires all raw milk cheeses to be aged sixty days or more.

AGED CHEESES ARE
(VIRTUALLY) LACTOSE-FREE

If you're cursed with lactose intolerance, I have good news for you: you can still eat cheese! During the cheesemaking process, the milk sugar known as lactose is either consumed by lactic acid during coagulation or drained away with the whey. As the cheese ages, the lactose disappears even more. Any cheeses aged two months or more, such as Gouda or Parmigiano, have the least amount of lactose. If you want to enjoy younger cheeses, just harness the power of Lactaid, which contains lactase, the enzyme needed to digest lactose.

HOW TO BUY CHEESE

The best place to buy cheese is at a cut-to-order cheese shop with cheesemongers who know how to properly care for the cheeses and can offer suggestions, samples, and pairing advice. A cheese counter like that is hard to come by, so if you're shopping at the grocery store, make sure you recognize the signs of deterioration. Cheese is sensitive to mishandling, especially soft-ripened cheeses like Bries. Look out for dents, cracks, dry patches, or any discoloration or molds that shouldn't be there on the interior paste. Be sure to check the label to ensure that the cheese was cut and wrapped within a week of purchasing and to look for specifics about the region, maker, and age of the cheese. The more a company reveals, the better: withholding details is a red flag that they've got something to hide. If you see PDO, AOC, DOP, or another similar acronym on a label, that means that the cheese is protected by a national government to preserve its history and production method.

"You have to be a romantic to invest yourself, your money, and your time, in cheese."

—ANTHONY BOURDAIN

THE PRICE OF CHEESE

Anthony Bourdain once said, "You have to be a romantic to invest yourself, your money, and your time in cheese." He was right. Making cheese is an arduous labor of love that requires long hours of backbreaking work. It takes a lot of money to care for the animals, purchase and maintain equipment, market and transport the product, or even operate a retail shop. While it's expensive for the consumer, there isn't a lot of profit left over for the ones who are doing the work. We devote our lives to cheese because we are romantics.

There are two types of cheese out there: the handmade artisanal variety and the mass-produced industrial kind. While the former costs considerably more, you're support-ing small artisans and ancient practices. The industrial food system is wreaking havoc on our planet, and it's our duty as cheese lovers to support those who are creating food in a way that respects the earth and her creatures.

On Plating Cheese

Transforming an array of wedges and accompaniments into a bountiful board can feel intimidating, but remember that all cheese plates are beautiful so long as you enjoy consuming them. Creating a cheese altar should be fun and celebratory rather than stressful. Of course, we all want a pretty platter, so take some inspiration from natural landscapes. Bisect your board with a winding trail of crackers, chip off a few crumbles that cascade from a mountain of Parmigiano-Reggiano, or gently fold prosciutto into a rippling stream. Here's a little step-by-step guide, in case you want a little more direction.

1 Turn on some music, take a deep meditative breath, and set aside enough time so you won't feel rushed.

2 Choose whatever platter or board fits the mood, and start by laying out any jars and bowls so you can build around their shapes.

3 Add the cheeses, evenly spacing the different types and arranging them from mild to strong.

4 Position accompaniments near their recommended cheese pairings to help guide people on where to begin. Fill in the gaps between the cheeses with loose items, like nuts, fruits, and chocolates.

5

Then, simply finish with garnishes and utensils.

WHEEL OF THE YEAR CHEESE PLATE
(clockwise from top)
A. Tomme Chèvre Grand-Mère Adrienne with cherry and almond crisps
B. Gabriel Coulet Roquefort with Hot Honey
C. Saint-Nectaire with blackberries
D. Pleasant Ridge Reserve from Uplands Cheese with roasted almonds. Sage and blood oranges to garnish.

Magic 101

As I've said before, you don't need to practice magic as you cook your way through this book. However, if you are interested in witchcraft, this is a great place to start. Don't be intimidated if you're at the beginning of your journey. Whether you've whispered a wish over birthday candles or simply spritzed yourself with your favorite perfume, you're already practicing magic. Just like with cheese, you don't need a lot of knowledge or tools to begin. If you trust your instincts, your palate, and yourself, the rest will fall into place.

PREPARING YOUR SPACE

To avoid bringing negative energy into your workings, it's important to cleanse your mind and clean your space before casting spells or performing other rituals. Take a few meditative breaths and then take a moment to prepare your space. Wipe down your counters, sweep your floors, and maybe even burn incense to clear away any lingering dark energies. Then gather your tools and ingredients so they're on hand as you cook. I also like to put on a playlist that aligns with my intention while I work.

HOW TO CAST A SPELL

1. Intention: Decide what it is you are trying to accomplish and set an intention to get it done. Try to get as clear and specific as possible. For example: If you're doing a money spell, write down the exact dollar amount that you're manifesting.

2. Invocation: Determine which energies you're invoking to achieve your desired result, using the correspondences on page 258 of this book. For example: If you're trying to cultivate self-love, cast your spell on a Friday, which is ruled by Venus, the planet of love. You can also work with rose petals, strawberries, and other Venusian ingredients. Make sure to speak words of gratitude for any and all energies that you invoke.

3. Action: This is the actual spellwork. Mix a drink, cook a recipe, or build a cheese plate. Speak your intention as you work, and express gratitude for the land, animals, and human hands that brought those ingredients to your kitchen. Complete the spell by enjoying the fruits of your labor.

4. Make It Your Own: At the end of this book, you'll find a list of Magical Correspondences that outlines herbs and other ingredients that will help you customize your spell. The list also features colors, numbers, planetary energies, and even the days of the week that will help you tailor your workings to your intentions.

TOOL KIT

- **Mortar and pestle** for grinding herbs and spices

- **Microplane** for zesting citrus and grating hard cheeses into a feathery dusting

- **Brûlée torch** for creating a caramelized sugar shell on fresh cheeses

- **Candy thermometer** for making hot honey

- **Scale** for measuring ingredients

- **Wooden spoons** can be used to direct energy into whatever it is you're stirring. They correspond with wands and can be charmed or carved with symbols. Since wood is porous, I recommend having one spoon for savory recipes and another for sweet, lest your honey-poached peaches stink of onions.

- **Kitchen knives** correspond with swords and ritual daggers, which are used to cut cords or remove psychological blocks. I recommend having a small, serrated blade for tomatoes, a longer serrated blade for cutting bread, a short paring knife for detailed jobs, and a chef's knife for heavy lifting.

- **Cheese knives** are mostly unnecessary, since you can cut most cheeses with a chef's knife. However, I do recommend having an offset blade or a cheese wire for getting a clean cut on delicate soft cheeses.

- **Miniature serving knives** are adorable and convenient for adorning cheese plates. If you don't have them, just use butter knives for soft cheeses and steak knives for harder wedges. If you want to invest in a set, I recommend one that has a spreader for soft cheese, a skeleton knife for semisoft to firm cheese, and a spear-tipped blade for hard cheese.

Magical Maintenance

Cleansing Your Tools
Simply wash with soap and water, while envisioning all energies and dirt rinsing away. Burn incense around them for additional cleansing.

Charging Your Tools
Speak an incantation to consecrate your tools. Make it personal and tailored to your intention. Then activate the tool by charging under the moon or sun. You can also anoint it with moon water (see recipe on page 19) or place it under a crystal.

CHEESE MAGIC PANTRY

- **Extra-virgin olive oil** for dressings and marinades

- **Neutral oil** for cooking at high temperatures

- **Good butter,** preferably unsalted, so you have more control over seasoning

- **Black pepper,** freshly ground

- **Honey,** preferably local and raw for best flavor and most medicinal qualities

- **Fresh lemons, limes, and oranges** because you can never have too much citrus

- **Vinegars,** specifically apple cider, balsamic, red wine, sherry, and champagne

- **Nuts,** preferably recently purchased since most will go rancid within three months (store them in the freezer to keep them extra fresh)

- **Whole spices** so you can grind them yourself with your mortar and pestle

- **Bouillon** or stock for that extra boost of flavor

The Kitchen Altar

An altar is a sacred space used to direct energy, honor deities, ground your workings, or just add a little bit of beauty into your life. I keep my altar in the center of my workspace and decorate it with a few crystals, an herb bundle for cleansing, a lighter, a bowl of seasonal fruit, and sometimes even fresh flowers when I'm feeling extra indulgent. I recommend making yours personal with a few trinkets or whatever items bring you inspiration. Keep it by your stove, among your salt and pepper, or by the sink to gaze at as you wash dishes after working your kitchen magic.

- **Fresh herbs** because dried ones just don't compare

- **Kosher salt** is less salty than table salt, which helps to thoroughly season your food. I developed the following recipes using Diamond Crystal Kosher Salt, which is about half as salty as Morton Salt. If you prefer Morton, I recommend halving the amount.

- **Flaky salt** for garnishing your food. There are different types, and they each serve a different purpose. Black salt is great for protection, pink salt is suited for love spells, and sea salt is the most versatile.

- **Moon water** for cleansing, charging, or using in potions and spellwork (see below)

MOON WATER RECIPE

To harness the power of the moon, fill a clean jar with water and place it outdoors or near a window overnight. In the morning, put a lid on it and store the jar in a dark place until ready to use.

You can make moon water during any moon phase, although I advise against doing so during eclipses. See the correspondences on page 258 for information about moon phases.

YULE

The festival of Yule marks the winter solstice.
The sun is reborn, and her waxing light has
overcome the cold, icy grip of the year's longest night.
The temperatures have dropped, and the world has
seemingly died all around us. We're in the midst of the
darkest part of the year, and yet Yule is a time of festivity,
gratitude, reflection, and light. We honor the great
evergreen, who retains her needles and reminds us that
life goes on even in the darkness. We celebrate new
beginnings and join together with our nearest
and dearest to feast, be merry, and welcome
the return of the sun and the start of a new year.

On or around June 21
✦ Southern Hemisphere ✦

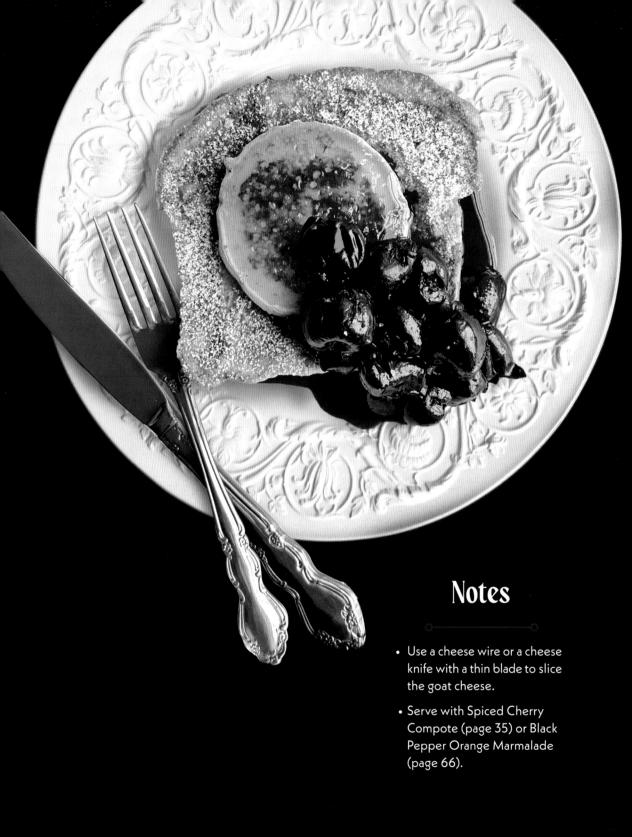

Notes

- Use a cheese wire or a cheese knife with a thin blade to slice the goat cheese.

- Serve with Spiced Cherry Compote (page 35) or Black Pepper Orange Marmalade (page 66).

Brûléed Bûcheron French Toast

SERVES 8

Crowned with a round of soft-ripened goat cheese that's sugared and torched with fire, this orange-infused French toast practically pulsates with solar energy. You can use any spongy, soft bread, such as challah, but just make sure it's a little stale so it can more easily soak up the batter. I recommend leaving it out overnight, but if you're limited on time, just lightly toast it. Pair with a pomander latte, using the syrup on page 39.

8 slices white bread, slightly stale or lightly toasted, cut ½ inch thick

4 large eggs

1 cup whole milk

2 tablespoons granulated sugar

Zest of 1 orange

½ teaspoon ground cardamom

¼ teaspoon cinnamon

¼ teaspoon ground cloves

1 teaspoon vanilla extract

½ teaspoon Diamond Crystal kosher salt

2 to 3 tablespoons salted butter for frying

6 to 8 ounces (170 g to 226 g) Bûcheron, Caña de Cabra, or other soft-ripened chèvre

4 teaspoons granulated sugar, for dusting

Confectioners' sugar, to serve

Preheat your oven to the lowest setting.

In a large bowl, whisk together the eggs and milk. Set aside.

In a small bowl, add the sugar, then add the orange zest and rub together with your fingers until the sugar is sandy and fragrant. Add the cardamom, cinnamon, cloves, vanilla, and salt and stir until combined.

Place one slice of bread in the batter, let it soak for about 1 minute, then flip to make sure it's fully saturated.

Melt a pat of butter in a pan over medium heat. Once it's foamy, add the battered bread and fry until golden brown, 4 to 5 minutes per side. Transfer to a sheet pan and set in the oven to keep warm until ready to serve. Repeat with the remaining slices.

Slice the goat cheese into 8 coins. Lay a coin onto each slice of French toast.

Sprinkle each slice with about ½ teaspoon of sugar. Use a brûlée torch to melt the sugar until until a brown crust forms.

Dust with confectioners' sugar and serve.

The Blue Cheese Yule Log

SERVES 6 TO 8

Here, we reinterpret the ancient tradition of the Yule log with a log-shaped cheese ball, dressed with chives for protection and infused with horseradish and hot sauce to symbolize the warmth of the returning sun. It's all coated with pecans and bacon to symbolize wealth (plus they make for very tasty bark). I recommend a mild, crumbly blue, such as buttermilk blue or Gorgonzola, and any tangy white cheddar aged no more than one year. Avoid anything pre-crumbled or pre-shredded, which can add odd flavors and mess up the texture. Pair with pale ale, champagne, or a Garlic Bloody Mary (page 106).

8 ounces (170 g) cream cheese, at room temperature

1 teaspoon jarred horseradish

1 teaspoon hot sauce

½ teaspoon Worcestershire sauce

¼ cup (20 g) chopped chives, divided

4 ounces (115 g) creamy blue cheese, such as buttermilk blue, freshly crumbled

4 ounces (115 g) white cheddar, freshly shredded

3 slices bacon, cooked, cooled, and chopped

¼ cup (25 g) roasted, unsalted pecans, chopped

Diamond Crystal kosher salt and freshly ground black pepper

Butter crackers and celery, to serve

In a medium bowl, add the cream cheese and a pinch of salt. Beat on low with an electric mixer until smooth. An electric mixer makes this very easy.

Whisk in the horseradish, hot sauce, Worcestershire, and 3 tablespoons of the chives.

Sprinkle the blue cheese, cheddar, and a pinch of black pepper over the mixture and stir to combine. Use your hands to shape into a log, cover with plastic wrap, and chill for 30 minutes or up to 2 days. (The longer it chills, the more the flavors will mix and mingle.)

When you're ready to serve, use a knife to gently carve your intention or wish for the year ahead into the log. Set aside.

On a large plate, add the bacon, pecans, and remaining chives and toss to mix well. Pat into an even layer.

Roll the log over the mixture, pressing gently all over to make the "bark" stick.

Serve with the crackers and celery.

Yule Log History

The burning of the Yule log is a Celtic ritual that uses sympathetic magic to lure back the sun and set intentions for the year ahead. Traditionally, a log of wood was carved with symbols or sigils, decorated with greenery, like holly or spruce, and lit aflame to represent the return of the light.

Notes

- You can substitute Pecorino, Parmigiano, or another hard, salty cheese for the Manchego.

- If you want less sweetness, leave out the dates.

Sunburst Radicchio Salad with Manchego

MAKES 2 TO 3 SERVINGS

This simple salad is crisp and bright, much like a perfect winter day. The radicchio represents the bitter cold, the orange reminds us of the waxing sunlight, and the crunchy texture brings healing energies. It's all finished with a simple, honey-kissed vinaigrette, a smattering of solar-ruled dates, and shaved Manchego.

FOR THE DRESSING
(makes ½ cup / 120 ml)

2 tablespoons white balsamic vinegar

1 teaspoon honey

Pinch of kosher salt

6 tablespoons extra-virgin olive oil

FOR THE SALAD

1 head radicchio, washed and dried, leaves separated

½ cup (120 ml) dressing

Kosher salt and freshly ground black pepper

½ fennel bulb, stalks and fronds removed

2 medium oranges

3 dates, pitted and roughly chopped

2 ounces (55 g) Manchego

Make the dressing: In a small bowl, whisk together the white balsamic, honey, and salt. Slowly drizzle in the olive oil, whisking continually until combined. Set aside.

Make the salad: Place the radicchio in a mixing bowl, and drizzle with ¼ cup of the dressing. Toss to coat, lightly massaging the leaves with your fingers as you meditate on the bitterness of winter. Season with salt and pepper to taste, then toss again.

Cut the core out of the fennel bulb, then slice as thinly as possible. Use a mandolin if you have one. Set aside.

Cut the peel off of the oranges, making sure no white pith remains. Slice into rounds, then cut the rounds into quarters. As you prepare the oranges, extend gratitude to the reborn sun. Set aside.

On a platter, lay out the radicchio and distribute the fennel and orange slices over top. Drizzle with the remaining dressing, and season with a pinch of salt. Sprinkle in the dates.

Using a vegetable peeler, shave the Manchego over the salad. Finish with a little more black pepper and serve.

Lucky Parm Beans with Garlic and Sage

SERVES 6 TO 8

While often discarded, the leftover rind of Parmigiano Reggiano is itself a magical ingredient, capable of infusing broths, soups, and stews with an unbeatable punch of rich, umami flavor. These lucky beans are also infused with garlic, red pepper flakes, and sage for added protective energy, health benefits, and flavor. Serve with crusty bread, an extra drizzle of olive oil, and a generous heap of grated Parm. Remember: the more Parm you add, the closer you are to another delicious rind—the cycle continues, the wheel turns.

- 1 pound (455 g) dried beans, such as cannellini or lima
- 4 sprigs sage, leaves removed and chopped
- 6 garlic cloves, peeled and chopped
- 2 tablespoons olive oil, plus more for serving
- 1 bay leaf
- 1 teaspoon red pepper flakes
- Freshly cracked black pepper
- 2 two-inch (5-cm) pieces Parmigiano rind
- 1 tablespoon Diamond Crystal kosher salt
- Lemon wedges, to serve
- Freshly grated Parm, to serve
- Crusty bread, to serve

Rinse the beans well (see Note). Add to a large mixing bowl and cover with 2 inches of water. Let soak for at least 4 hours or up to 12.

Drain the water and transfer the beans to a large pot. Cover with 2 inches of water.

Add the sage, garlic, olive oil, bay leaf, red pepper flakes, and several cracks of black pepper. Stir three times and envision your year ahead filling with wealth and health. Bring to a simmer over medium-low heat.

Drop the rinds into the pot and stir three times. Cover and let cook until the beans are al dente. This will take anywhere from 30 to 90 minutes, depending on the type of beans you're using and how old they are.

Add the kosher salt and stir three times. Cook until the beans are just tender, then taste and season as needed.

Remove the rind, and discard. Ladle the beans into a bowl with plenty of broth. Drizzle with more olive oil, squeeze the lemon wedges over top, and finish with grated Parm and more black pepper. Serve with the bread.

Notes

- Make sure to use authentic Parmigiano-Reggiano or Grana Padano. Their production standards are protected by the Italian government, so their quality is guaranteed, unlike cheaper imitations, which often lack the same depth of flavor.

- Beans are associated with luck, wealth, and prosperity. You can use any dried bean you have on hand, but I prefer creamy white beans like cannellinis. I use Christmas lima beans, because they're beautiful and festive. I strongly discourage using canned beans, which will get mushy before they properly infuse the flavors.

- Wash your beans well before soaking, to rinse away debris and pebbles hiding in the mix. I recommend placing them inside a large bowl or pot and filling it with water. Swirl them around a little, drain, and repeat until the water is clear.

Notes

- For the best flavor, start with raw, whole pistachios and shell them yourself. Then roast them in a dry pan over medium-low heat for about 10 minutes, stirring occasionally.

- Store bark in an airtight container in the fridge and eat within 2 weeks. You can also freeze it for up to 3 months.

Bejeweled White Chocolate Bark with Goat Gouda

SERVES 6 TO 8

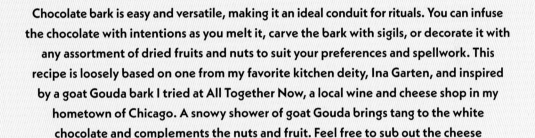

Chocolate bark is easy and versatile, making it an ideal conduit for rituals. You can infuse the chocolate with intentions as you melt it, carve the bark with sigils, or decorate it with any assortment of dried fruits and nuts to suit your preferences and spellwork. This recipe is loosely based on one from my favorite kitchen deity, Ina Garten, and inspired by a goat Gouda bark I tried at All Together Now, a local wine and cheese shop in my hometown of Chicago. A snowy shower of goat Gouda brings tang to the white chocolate and complements the nuts and fruit. Feel free to sub out the cheese as long as it's hard and easy to grate.

8 ounces (230 g) high-quality white chocolate, roughly chopped

1 ounce (28 g) goat Gouda

¼ cup (25 g) roasted and salted pistachios, roughly chopped

¼ cup (40 g) dried cherries

½ teaspoon flaky salt

Add ¾ of the white chocolate to a heatproof glass bowl and microwave for 20 seconds. Stir well with a rubber spatula, and microwave another 20 seconds. Repeat, heating in 10 second intervals, until melted. Add the rest of the chocolate, and stir until completely smooth.

Line a sheet pan with parchment paper. Pour the chocolate over the paper, using a rubber spatula to spread it evenly, leaving a 2-inch (5-cm) border.

Using a microplane, grate the Gouda over the chocolate. It should resemble freshly fallen snow.

Decorate the bark with the pistachios and dried cherries. Gently press the toppings into the bark so they stick. Finish with a light sprinkling of the salt.

Let cool for about an hour, then break into shards and serve.

Marinated Olives

MAKES ABOUT 2 CUPS (350 G)

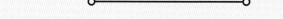

Olives are native to the Mediterranean and have long been used in religious rituals. Prized for their healing antioxidant properties, olives are associated with the Sun. Here, they're warmed in their own oil and steeped with two other solar foods: rosemary and oranges. Garlic and red pepper flakes infuse the oil with their protective energies and savory heat. This ritual is a perfect way to honor the sun's rebirth and transform basic olives into a luxurious accompaniment for aged sheep's milk cheeses and a Perfect Martini (page 216).

½ cup (120 ml) extra-virgin olive oil

¼ orange, thinly sliced into quarter wheels

2 garlic cloves, peeled and smashed

2 small sprigs rosemary

Pinch of red pepper flakes

1 cup (175 g) high-quality, unpitted olives, either a mix or a specific type like Picholine, Kalamata, or Castelvetrano

In a medium saucepan, warm the olive oil over low heat.

Add the orange, garlic, rosemary, and red pepper flakes.

Bring to a sizzle over medium-low heat and cook for 5 minutes. Add the olives.

Turn off the heat and let sit for about 15 minutes.

Serve warm, alongside a bowl for pits.

Note

If you're planning to store these
for a while, substitute ¼ cup
(60 ml) of olive oil with
grapeseed oil to prevent the
mixture from solidifying in the
fridge. The olives will last about
1 month when refrigerated and
stored in an airtight container.

Spiced Cherry Compote

MAKES ABOUT 1 CUP (200 G)

Yule is a time to celebrate the return of the sun with those you love, and this cherry compote is the perfect offering to them. Cherries are traditionally linked with love, especially when plumped in a warm bath of lemon juice, sugar, vanilla, and fiery mulling spices. Jar it up for homemade gifts or serve with festive cheeses such as triple-cream Brie, Alpine styles, and creamy blues. When the cherries are gone, mix the leftover syrup with seltzer for a delicious spritz.

5 black peppercorns

3 whole cloves

10 ounces (280 g) frozen Bing cherries, pitted

1 tablespoon lemon juice

1 ½ tablespoons granulated sugar

¼ teaspoon Diamond Crystal kosher salt

1 cinnamon stick

½ teaspoon vanilla extract

Place the peppercorns and cloves in a mortar. Crush with your pestle, as you visualize the warmth and festivity of the season. Set aside.

In a saucepan, combine the cherries, lemon juice, peppercorns, cloves, sugar, salt, and cinnamon stick.

Cook over medium. Once the cherries release their juices and begin to simmer, reduce to medium-low and cook, stirring occasionally, until the cherries soften, about 15 minutes. Turn off the heat. Add the vanilla and stir to combine.

Let cool for 10 minutes, then pour into an 8-ounce (240-ml) jar or other vessel if serving immediately. If not, store in a sealed container in the fridge for about 1 week.

Ginger Drop Cookies

MAKES ABOUT 3 DOZEN, DEPENDING ON COOKIE SIZE

Gingerbread has deep roots that span the globe. Ginger is native to Southeast Asia, where it's prized for its medicinal properties. Gingerbread can be traced back to the ceremonial honey cakes of ancient Egypt, Greece, and Rome. As spice trading developed into the Middle Ages, Europeans began incorporating the newly available spices into their baked goods. Eventually, ginger-spiked breads, cakes, and cookies became essential festival fare, especially during Yule. I associate ginger cookies with my Norwegian ancestors, which is exactly where this recipe comes from. Serve them on the Yule Cookie Offering Plate (page 44) with aged Gouda or a rich, creamy blue cheese.

¾ cup (190 g) vegetable shortening, such as Crisco

1 ¼ cup (250 g) granulated sugar, divided

1 large egg

¼ cup (80 g) molasses (see Note)

2 teaspoons baking soda

2 cups (240 g) flour

1 teaspoon ground ginger

¼ teaspoon ground cloves

½ teaspoon kosher salt

2 teaspoons ground cinnamon

Preheat the oven to 325°F (160°C). Line two baking sheets with parchment paper or silicone baking mats. Set aside.

In a large bowl, cream together the shortening and 1 cup (200 g) of the sugar using an electric mixer. Add the egg and beat until combined.

Add the molasses and baking powder to a separate small bowl and stir until fully combined. Add the molasses mixture to the batter and beat until incorporated.

In a separate bowl, combine the flour, ginger, cloves, and salt. Add to the mixture and beat to incorporate.

Cover and let chill in the refrigerator for 30 minutes.

Roll the dough into balls, working with about a teaspoon at a time. In a small bowl, mix together the rest of the sugar and the cinnamon. Dip each ball into the cinnamon sugar mix, and transfer to the baking sheet, about 2 inches apart.

Bake for about 12 minutes, until they're golden brown but still a little soft in the middle. Transfer to a wire rack to cool completely.

Notes

- You can substitute butter for the vegetable shortening, but it's just not the same. My ancestors migrated to the Midwest from Germany, so this is how I honor the American side of my heritage.

- Don't use blackstrap molasses—it's much too dark and intense for these cookies.

Note

- If you want a stronger-flavored syrup, pour the unstrained syrup into an airtight container and let the spices steep for 24 hours. Strain before using.

Pomander Old-Fashioned

MAKES 1 COCKTAIL

Pomanders are a classic Christmas decoration, featuring whole oranges that are studded with cloves and hung to dry. These beautiful, fragrant balls originated in medieval Europe where they were used to ward off illnesses believed to be caused by inhaling foul odors. Eventually, witches adapted the pomanders into a charm for protection, health, and good luck. Here, the flavors of orange peel and cloves perfume the simple syrup in this festive old-fashioned. I've also added star anise, which imbues the syrup with more protective energies and a subtle licorice-y scent. For a nonalcoholic beverage, use the syrup in a latte or chai. Serve alongside the aged Alpine-style and spruce-wrapped cheeses featured on the Cheese Wreath Plate (page 43).

FOR THE POMANDER SYRUP

1 orange

½ cup (100 g) light brown sugar

½ cup (100 g) granulated sugar

¼ teaspoon Diamond Crystal kosher salt

20 whole cloves (about ¾ teaspoon ground)

1 star anise pod

FOR THE OLD-FASHIONED

2.5 ounces (75 ml) bourbon or rye

3 dashes Angostura bitters

½ ounce (30 ml) pomander syrup

Strip of orange peel , to garnish

Make the syrup: Cut off the orange peel, being careful to avoid the pith. Set aside the orange flesh for another use.

In a small saucepan, bring 1 cup (240 ml) water to a simmer over medium heat. Add the orange peel, both sugars, and salt, and stir to combine.

Add the cloves and star anise to a mortar, and lightly crush with a pestle while asking the universe for protection during the harsh winter.

Add the crushed cloves and star anise to the saucepan, reduce to a simmer, and cook for 10 minutes. Let cool for 10 minutes, then strain. The syrup will last about 2 weeks when stored in an airtight container in the refrigerator.

Make the cocktail: Fill a mixing glass with ice. Add the bourbon or rye, bitters, and syrup. Stir for 30 seconds.

Put a large ice cube into a rocks glass, then strain the cocktail over the ice. Squeeze the orange peel over and drop into the glass.

Midwinter Spritz

MAKES 1 COCKTAIL

This spin on the classic Aperol Spritz is made with cranberry to protect you throughout the year ahead and garnished with lime to purify the one that's passed. Aperol is a citrusy potion made from rhubarb and a secret blend of herbs and roots. This bitter aperitif brings a festive red hue and an herbaceous complexity that pairs well with a lot of cheeses, especially the ones on the New Year's Platter (page 46). There are a lot of nonalcoholic versions of Aperol, so absolutely feel free to substitute and adjust the other ingredients to taste. Pair it with an aged sheep's milk cheese or a soft-ripened goat cheese.

3 ounces (90 ml) prosecco, cava, or seltzer

2 ounces (60 ml) cranberry juice

1 ounce (60 ml) Aperol, or a nonalcoholic aperitif

1 lime slice, to garnish

Fill a wineglass with ice and pour the prosecco over. Add the cranberry juice and Aperol, and stir to incorporate. Garnish with the lime slice and serve.

The Battle of Holly and Oak

One of the most famous legends surrounding the solstice is the ancient Druidic lore of Holly and Oak, which personifies the cycle of death and rebirth. Throughout the year, the Holly and Oak kings battle for supremacy. The Holly King prevails at the summer solstice, bringing destruction and darkness as the sunlight wanes and the earth dies. At the winter solstice, however, the Oak King wins and initiates rebirth and renewal with the waxing sunlight.

Some believe that the Holly King was the original inspiration for Saint Nicholas, since he's often depicted in red with holly sprigs in his cap and a team of eight reindeer. Others believe that Santa derived from the Nordic god Odin, who rode an eight-legged horse and gave gifts to his favored followers. Odin's sons Baldr and Hodr, also star in the Nordic myth that echoes that of the Holly and Oak kings.

ROSEMARY
FLATBREADS
complement the woodsy
notes in the spruce-
wrapped cheese and
serve as a dipping vessel.

THE CHEESE WREATH PLATE

BAY LEAVES
AND ROSEMARY

both represent sun energy
and charge the plate with
protective powers.

For more than 4,000 years, people have used wreaths to represent the Wheel of the Year and the sun's rebirth on the winter solstice. This cheese wreath embodies this ancient symbol with two solar-powered cheeses: an aged Alpine-style made with summer milk and a luscious, bark-wrapped cheese that's created in the fall and winter. The pairing honors traditional Alpine cheesemaking practices. Comté, Gruyère, and other Alpine styles come in huge wheels, which require a lot of milk. In the fall, the cows switch from feasting on fresh Alpine grass to dried hay, which makes for richer milk and a lower yield. Since there isn't enough milk to make the big wheels, cheese-makers make Vacherin Mont d'Or, a smaller cheese that's so soft it needs a belt of spruce bark to keep the shape, lest she ooze out of her rind.

1 Summer milk Alpine-style

cheeses are literally charged by the sun. Look for Pleasant Ridge Reserve from Uplands Cheese (featured), Gruyère Alpage, or summer-milk Comté.

2 Spruce-wrapped

cheeses have a festive decadence and the aura of a winter-kissed forest. I recommend a seasonal, raw milk version such as Rush Creek Reserve from Uplands Cheese (featured), Vach-erin Mont d'Or, or Winnimere from Jasper Hill Farm in Vermont. Harbison is a wonderful option that's available year-round from Jasper Hill Farm.

POMEGRANATE
SEEDS
add pops of
festive red.

THINLY SLICED
CURED MEATS
such as coppa or
soppressata, bring salty
savor and adorn the
wreath like ribbons.

WHOLE-GRAIN
MUSTARD
embodies the element of
fire and complements the
earthy, funky flavors in
the wreath.

1 Aged Goudas

glitter with crunchy crystals and bring candy-sweet toffee notes that complement candied pecans. All Goudas are made by rinsing and scalding the curds, which creates a sweeter cheese that can age for a long time. Younger wheels are mild and flexible, while older cheeses develop a flaky, toothsome texture with festive notes of figs and butterscotch. Any aged Gouda will do, but my favorites are L'Amuse Signature Gouda, Beemster XO (featured), and OG Kristal from Belgium.

2 Triple cream Bries

are enriched with added cream, resulting in a spreadable texture akin to whipped butter. They're a decadent topping for crunchy pizzelle, especially with a dollop of cherry compote. Try Délice de Bourgogne (featured), Saint Angel, or Trillium from Tulip Tree Creamery in Indianapolis.

3 Creamy blues

are a lovely match to spicy Ginger Drop Cookies. Their rich, luscious fats help your taste buds access all of the flavors, while the pungent blue notes complement the spices. Blue cheeses are always extra salty, which helps the molds proliferate, so molasses-sweet baked goods tend to mellow their salinity. Look for something mild and spreadable, like Cambozola Black Label (featured), Cashel Blue, or Bleu d'Auvergne.

PIZZELLE

are Italian wafer cookies traditionally served on holidays and pressed with beautiful, intricate designs reminiscent of snowflakes.

BEJEWELED WHITE CHOCOLATE BARK WITH GOAT GOUDA

(page 31) brings the traditional Yule colors against a snow-white backdrop.

BAY LEAVES

represent sun energy and add a pop of festive green.

BOURBON-GLAZED PECANS

(page 213) offer fiery spices and a kiss of woodsy bourbon flavor.

SPICED CHERRY COMPOTE

(page 35) brings rich, jubilant flavors that pair with all these cheeses and cookies.

GINGER DROP COOKIES

(page 36) bring the power of ginger, a sacred root for Greco-Roman solar deities.

2

THE YULE COOKIE OFFERING PLATE

Making cookies is perhaps the most common food ritual during Yuletide. The traditional cookie swap comes from an old Germanic pagan custom of gifting friends and family with baked treats to call in a sweet, prosperous new year. Of course, there's also the practice of leaving cookies for Santa, which stems from offering sweets and baked goods to gods and goddesses in exchange for protection and abundant crops in the coming year. In Italy, it's tradition to leave out cakes and cookies for La Befana, a gift-giving witch who visits children the night before the Feast of the Epiphany. Cheese and cookies also complement each other beautifully and make for a festive, celebratory platter. Pair with hot cocoa, coffee, mulled wine, or the Pomander Old-Fashioned (page 39).

3

THE NEW YEAR'S PLATTER

MARCONA ALMONDS are associated with wealth, especially because they're fried and salted.

ROE brings energies of wealthy and fertility, blessing your new year with joy and success in all endeavors.

While many witches welcome their new year at Samhain (aka Halloween), much of the world celebrates with the Gregorian calendar. My favorite part about New Year's Eve is the opportunity to celebrate with decadence: champagne, caviar, gold, and glitter! It's Yule's last hurrah: an opportunity to gather your loved ones and bid farewell to what's come to pass and what's yet to come. This New Year's Platter serves up a plethora of indulgent flavors that correspond to the sun and call in wealth, health, and protection during yet another turn of the wheel. Serve with champagne, Pomegranate Tonic (page 246), or Midwinter Spritz (page 40).

MANDARINS represent the sun and are traditionally eaten at the lunar new year to bring good luck and happiness.

BLINIS are a traditional caviar accompaniment and are made with buckwheat, which attracts abundance.

BAY LEAVES offer sun energy and manifest wealth in the new year.

MARINATED OLIVES (page 32) are solar-powered and pair particularly well with the aged sheep's milk cheese.

2

FENNEL TARALLI

are crunchy, breadstick-like crackers that are shaped into rings, representing the Wheel of the Year.

FIGS

symbolize strength and bring a welcome sweet contrast against the savory flavors of the plate.

3

GREEN GRAPES

are another lucky symbol, especially in Spain, where it's tradition to eat twelve while sitting under a table to bring fortune to each month of the new year.

1

Mascarpone

is a luscious, spreadable Italian fresh cheese that's sort of like the richer, more sophisticated cousin to cream cheese. She's silky and milky sweet with a fluffy texture nearly as voluminous as whipped cream. Though she's often found in sweet desserts like tiramisu, she also serves as an ideal topping for blinis or a bed for caviar.

2

Idiazábal

is Spain's most popular cheese second to Manchego. She's made in the Basque and Navarre regions using raw milk exclusively from Latxa sheep. Historically, the wheels were made in the mountains during the summer season and dried fireside, where they developed a smoky flavor. Nowadays not all wheels are smoked, but Idiazábal has a distinctly savory flavor from the use of animal rennet. Pair with almonds and olives.

3

Humboldt Fog

is one of the most iconic cheeses in America. Tart and herbaceous with notes of pink peppercorns near the rind, she pairs well with the fennel and citrus. You can also substitute another soft-ripened goat's milk cheese like Valençay or Caña de Cabra.

IMBOLC

Marking the halfway point between the winter solstice and spring equinox, the ancient Celtic festival of Imbolc celebrates the end of winter's darkest days. It's a time for planting seeds for future harvest, but it's also an ideal cheese holiday because of its association with sheep's milk. Some historians believe the name is derived from *Imbolg*, which is Old Irish for "in the belly." This refers to lambing season, when the sheep give birth, beginning their lactation cycle and the cheesemaking season. Other experts believe the name comes from *oimelc*, which means "ewe's milk." Either way, Imbolc celebrates hope and the promise of spring.

August 1 to 2
✦ Southern Hemisphere ✦

Note

Make sure the macaroni isn't fridge cold. Zap in the microwave for 30-second intervals or let temper for 30 minutes before cooking.

Mac-and-Cheese Frittata

SERVES 4

A freshly baked batch of mac and cheese is spellbinding, until you try to reheat the leftovers and find yourself cursed with an oily mess. Luckily, I created a hack by way of the blessed pasta frittata. This is a dish of necessity: all you need are eggs, pasta sauce to add a little acidity, macaroni and cheese, and a little extra shredded cheese as a finishing touch. This resourceful little meal makes for an ideal breakfast, lunch, or dinner, especially alongside some lightly dressed greens. Feel free to use any leftover mac and cheese you have on hand, whether from a box, restaurant, or homemade using the recipe on page 206.

6 large eggs

½ teaspoon Diamond Crystal kosher salt

Freshly ground black pepper

2 teaspoons unsalted butter

10 to 12 ounces (285 g to 340 g) leftover macaroni and cheese, at room temperature

½ cup (125 ml) marinara or other tomato sauce

½ cup (50 g) melting cheese such as Gruyère, mozzarella, or fontina (even a mix of whatever was used in the original recipe), freshly shredded

Preheat the oven to 350°F (175°C).

In a medium bowl, whisk the eggs together with the salt and a few cracks of black pepper. Set aside.

In a 9-inch ovenproof skillet over medium-low heat, melt the butter. Spoon the leftover macaroni into the skillet, making sure it's in an evenly distributed layer. Pour the eggs over, making sure all the macaroni is well covered.

Let cook until the frittata pulls away from the sides of the pan, about 5 to 7 minutes.

Swirl the marinara on top, and carve with any sigils, symbols, or runes you'd like.

Sprinkle the cheese over and finish with another crack of black pepper. Transfer to the oven and bake until the cheese is melted and the frittata is fully set, about 15 minutes. Remove from the oven.

Let cool for 10 minutes. Serve warm or at room temperature.

Cover and store in the fridge for up to 5 days.

Burrata with Chili Crisp and Scallions

SERVES 4 TO 6

Most of us don't have access to a lot of fresh seasonal produce in the middle of winter, and that's when we must make magic out of simple pantry staples. This spicy appetizer needs only chili crisp, honey, scallions, and a sprinkle of flaky salt. It's brimming with fierce fire powers to speed up our reawakening from winter's slumber. Both chilis and alliums like scallions are ruled by Mars and can ward off malevolent energy, while the honey brings solar powers. You can use burrata or stracciatella, which are the cream-soaked shreds of mozzarella that make up burrata's filling. Pair with crunchy crostini and a crisp pilsner or lime soda.

8 ounces (225 g) burrata or stracciatella

2 teaspoons chili crisp

1 teaspoon honey

1 scallion, dark parts removed and thinly sliced

Flaky salt and freshly ground black pepper

Crostini, to serve

Place the burrata on a serving platter and cut it in half. Pull the two halves apart gently, spreading out the innards a little bit.

In a small bowl, whisk together the chili crisp and honey, and drizzle over the burrata. Sprinkle the scallions evenly over the cheese. Finish with a big pinch of flaky salt and freshly ground black pepper.

Serve with crostini.

Beets and blue cheese are one of those enchanted couplings: they complement each other's earthiness, while the sweet beets provide contrast to the salty blue. You can use any blue cheese for this, but I recommend a rindless variety such as Roquefort, Maytag Blue, Bleu d'Auvergne, or Point Reyes Original Blue, which is my personal preference here.

Blue Cheese and Beet Salad with Seeded Gravel

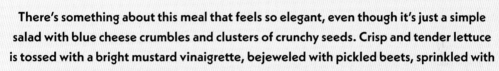

SERVES 4

There's something about this meal that feels so elegant, even though it's just a simple salad with blue cheese crumbles and clusters of crunchy seeds. Crisp and tender lettuce is tossed with a bright mustard vinaigrette, bejeweled with pickled beets, sprinkled with Seeded Gravel, and finished with crumbles of blue cheese. It's best enjoyed for lunch with a glass of chilled white wine, but ginger ale also makes for a delightful pairing.

FOR THE DRESSING

2 tablespoons sherry vinegar

1 teaspoon Dijon mustard

1 tablespoon honey

Kosher salt and black pepper

¼ cup (60 ml) extra-virgin olive oil

FOR THE SALAD

6 cups (282 g) tender green lettuce, washed and dried

Salt and freshly ground black pepper

1 ½ cups (255g) pickled beets (page 65)

½ cup (72 g) Seeded Gravel (page 62)

3 ounces (85 g) blue cheese, crumbled

Make the dressing: In a small bowl, whisk together the vinegar, mustard, honey, and a pinch of kosher salt and freshly ground black pepper. Slowly drizzle in the olive oil, whisking constantly, until it's fully emulsified. Set aside.

Make the salad: Add the lettuce to a large mixing bowl. Add half of the dressing. Toss to coat. Season with a pinch of salt and toss again. Taste a leaf to test seasoning and adjust as needed.

Pile the dressed lettuce onto four plates and top with the beets. Drizzle with the remaining dressing and season with salt and pepper. Sprinkle the Seeded Gravel and crumbled blue cheese over top.

Raclette Bread Pudding with Caramelized Cabbage and Caraway

SERVES 6

For our ancestors, resources were scarce in the middle of winter. Any available food was precious, and they couldn't let anything go to waste. This bread pudding honors their resourcefulness, making magic out of stale bread and commonly cellared cabbage and onions. The vegetables are cooked down and caramelized with caraway and thyme, all of which carry powerful protective energies to guard you through winter's end. Pair with a robust red wine, black tea, or a malty Belgian ale.

1 pound (454 g) sourdough bread

2 tablespoons unsalted butter, plus more for buttering the baking dish

½ yellow onion, thinly sliced

2 garlic cloves

1 teaspoon caraway seeds

1 cabbage, sliced into ribbons

1 tablespoon fresh thyme leaves, chopped

14 ounces (400 g) raclette, divided

2½ cups (600 ml) whole milk

6 large eggs

½ teaspoon Diamond Crystal kosher salt

Black pepper

Cut the bread into cubes. Spread it out evenly on a baking sheet or cutting board and let sit for a couple of hours until stale.

Generously butter a 9 x 12-inch (22 x 30 cm) baking dish. Set aside.

In a large skillet over medium-low heat, melt the 2 tablespoons of butter. Add the onion and cook until soft and fragrant, about 5 minutes. Add the thyme and caraway and stir. Cook for 5 minutes, stirring occasionally.

Add the cabbage all at once. (It will seem like a lot at first, but it cooks down very quickly.)

Cook, stirring occasionally, until the cabbage is deeply caramelized, about 45 minutes to an hour. Stir in the garlic, cook another 3 minutes. Remove from the heat. Let cool for 10 minutes.

(continued on page 58)

Note

The star ingredient is Raclette, a stanky little Alpine cheese that melts like a dream and infuses the pudding with her savory, meaty flavor.

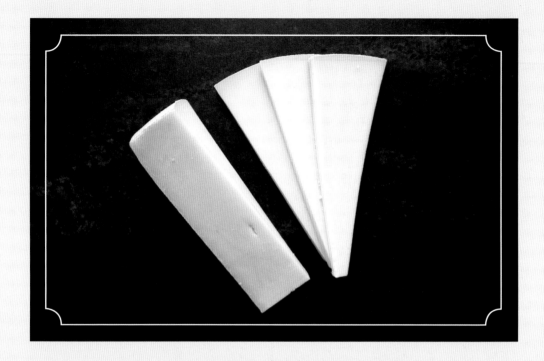

RACLETTE BREAD PUDDING WITH CARAMELIZED
CABBAGE AND CARAWAY, *continued*

Measure out a cup of cabbage and toss with half of the cheese and all of the bread. Layer evenly inside the baking dish.

Whisk together the milk, eggs, salt, and a couple cracks of black pepper and pour over the cabbage and bread mixture. Stir, making sure the bread cubes are thoroughly coated. Cover tightly, refrigerate, and let soak for at least 4 hours, or preferably, overnight.

When you're ready to cook, preheat the oven to 325°F (160°C). Top the dish with the rest of the cabbage and cheese. Bake for about an hour, or until the cheese is browned and a knife comes out clean in the center.

Let cool for 10 to 15 minutes. Serve warm.

Brigid, the Celtic Fire Goddess

One of the
most iconic figures of
Imbolc is Brigid, the Celtic sun
goddess of poetry, smithcraft, inspiration,
and healing. She is a guardian of children
and protector of the home against fire—she is
often depicted over a cauldron to represent the
powers of inspiration and creativity that burn within
each of us. Her followers are known to leave Brigid
offerings of coins in one of Ireland's many springs
and wells (the origins behind the modern ritual of
throwing a penny in a fountain while making a wish).
Her sacred food is blackberries, and her followers
often honor her with a Brigid's cross, which is made
of woven straw or rushes. With the Christianization
of the Celts, Brigid was turned into a saint and
Imbolc was rechristened Candlemas.

Raspberry Brie Love Tarts

MAKES 16 PASTRIES

These bewitching pastries are filled with sunny orange marmalade and warm, melted Brie. Each tart is crowned with Venus-ruled raspberries, lush with red juices that represent the heart's blood. Some say these berries' brambles can even heal a broken heart or fortify a struggling partnership. I don't know if that's true, but I can tell you that these Love Tarts are incredibly easy to make, which gives even novice bakers a sense of empowerment. What's sexier than confidence?

14-ounce (400 g) package puff pastry, thawed

⅓ cup (80 ml) Black Pepper Orange Marmalade (page 66)

1 large egg, beaten

6 ounces (170 g) mild Brie, at room temperature

8-ounce (230 g) container raspberries, washed and dried

Flaky salt, to garnish

Confectioners' sugar, for dusting

Preheat the oven to 400°F (200°C). Line two baking sheets with parchment paper or a silicone mat and set aside.

Gently unfold the puff pastry onto a cutting board. Cut into 8 even rectangles, roughly 2½ x 3 inches (6 x 7 cm).

Using a paring knife, gently score a square inside each, leaving about ¼-inch (6-mm) trim. Prick the inside of the square with a fork.

Drop a teaspoon of marmalade into the center of each pastry and spread evenly inside the square. Brush the edges with the beaten egg.

Transfer the tarts to the baking sheets and bake until puffed and golden, about 13 to 15 minutes.

While the tarts are in the oven, slice the Brie into 16 pieces.

Remove the tarts from the oven. Place one slice of Brie inside each pastry. Return to the oven and bake until the Brie is just melted, about 2 to 3 minutes.

Remove from the oven and let cool for a few minutes. Place 3 raspberries on top of each pastry, and sprinkle with the flaky salt. Let cool for 5 more minutes, and dust with confectioners' sugar. Serve and enjoy!

Seeded Gravel

MAKES 1½ CUPS (150 G)

Imbolc is a time for planting seeds for the future harvest. This seeded gravel is essentially a savory granola meets abundance ritual. It's filled with pepitas for prosperity, sesame seeds for wealth, and sunflower seeds for happiness and creativity. Paprika and black pepper offer protection and heat, for calling back your magic and speeding up your spell. Sprinkle over the Blue Cheese and Beet Salad (page 55) for an extra boost of magic.

¼ cup (30 g) pepitas

¼ cup (30 g) sunflower seeds

2 tablespoons black sesame seeds

1 tablespoon unsalted butter, melted

½ tablespoon Hot Honey (page 130)

½ teaspoon Diamond Crystal kosher salt

¼ teaspoon freshly ground black pepper

¼ teaspoon paprika

Preheat the oven to 350°F (175°C). Line a baking sheet with parchment paper or a silicone mat.

In a medium bowl, stir together the pepitas, sunflower seeds, and sesame seeds.

In a separate bowl, mix together the butter, honey, salt, pepper, and paprika.

Pour over the seeds and stir to coat, envisioning the energies of happiness, abundance, and protection mingling and amplifying each another.

Spread the coated seeds onto the baking sheet in an even layer.

Bake until golden and crisp, about 10 to 12 minutes. Let cool completely and break into crumbles.

Pickled Beets

SERVES 6 TO 8

Beets are associated with passion and matters of the heart, due to their blood-red hue. The ancient Greeks believed that Aphrodite ate beets to amplify her beauty. They're also shown to improve your mood, relax your mind, and even lower your blood pressure. These tender, pickled beets are also infused with thyme and caraway, which also share an association with Aphrodite. Serve them with oranges and fresh chèvre, or in the Blue Cheese and Beet Salad on page 55.

1 pound (455 g) beets, scrubbed

1 teaspoon olive oil

½ shallot, sliced

½ cup (120 ml) white vinegar

½ cup (120 ml) cider vinegar

⅓ cup (70 g) granulated sugar

2 sprigs fresh thyme

½ teaspoon caraway seeds

1 teaspoon Diamond Crystal kosher salt

Preheat the oven to 350°F (175°C).

Add the beets to a roasting pan in a single layer. Drizzle with olive oil and about ¼ cup (60 ml) of water. Cover the pan with foil and roast until the beets are fork-tender, about 45 minutes to an hour depending on their size.

Once cooked, let the beets cool, and peel off the skins with your fingers. If the peels are stubborn, use a paring knife.

Chop the beets into 1-inch (2.5 cm) pieces and transfer to a jar with the shallot.

In a medium saucepan over medium heat, combine 1 cup (240 ml) of water and the vinegars, cover, and bring to a boil.

Stir in the sugar, thyme, caraway, and salt. Simmer for 10 minutes.

Turn off the heat and pour the brine over the beets. Let cool to room temperature, then close the jar. Shake it to combine, then place in the refrigerator for a day. Pickled beets will last about a month in the fridge.

Black Pepper Orange Marmalade

MAKES 1½ QUARTS (1.4 L)

Making marmalade is a labor of love. It takes time and patience to thinly slice the fruit, macerate it in syrup, and simmer it down until it's thick and sticky. This is a fitting activity for a cold winter's day: a bit of sympathetic magic to lure back the sun and call in the arrival of spring. Oranges are also at their best in winter, and there's more variety available. Sevilles make the best marmalade, but you can also use navel, Cara Cara, or even blood oranges. The addition of black pepper brings a heat and a protective fiery energy that amplifies the purifying powers of the oranges. Serve with soft-ripened goat cheeses on the Ostara Brunch Plate (page 108) or with the Lemon Poppy Seed Goat Cheese Scones (page 82).

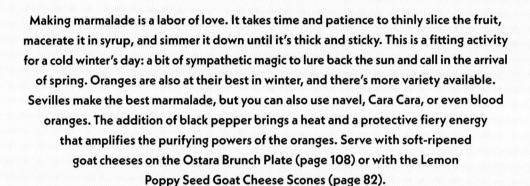

2 large seedless oranges (about 1½ pounds / 680 g)

1 lemon (about ¼ pound / 115 g)

4 cups (960 ml) water

4 cups (800 g) granulated sugar

2 teaspoons freshly ground black pepper

1 teaspoon Diamond Crystal kosher salt

Slice the oranges and lemon in half lengthwise. Then thinly slice into half-moons. Discard any seeds.

Transfer the citrus and any juices to a large stockpot.

Pour in the water and bring to a boil. Add the sugar and stir until it dissolves. Turn off the heat and let sit at room temperature for 8 hours or overnight.

The next day, place a small plate in your freezer.

Add the black pepper to a dry pan, and heat over medium heat. Let toast, stirring occasionally, for about 2 minutes.

Add the black pepper and salt to the orange mixture, and bring back to a boil. Reduce to a simmer and cook for 90 minutes, stirring occasionally and visualizing the waxing sunlight thawing the cold earth.

(continued on page 68)

BLACK PEPPER ORANGE MARMALADE, *continued*

Turn the heat back up to a boil. Cook for 30 minutes. As it boils, use a spoon to mash up any large chunks. Make sure to skim off any foam that rises to the top.

Once the marmalade is pulpy but still loose, check if it's done by putting a spoonful on the frozen plate. If the marmalade holds its shape once it cools, then it's ready. If it seems runny, then let it cook for 5 minutes longer and check again. If it's too hard, then add a little hot water.

Let cool, then scrape into a couple clean 12-ounce (355 ml) mason jars. Chill in the fridge overnight. It will keep for about a month.

This technique is based on Anna's Orange Marmalade, as published by my queen, Ina Garten.

Winter Divination

Most Americans are familiar with Groundhog Day, when Punxsutawney Phil peeks his head out of his hole to see if we'll have six more weeks of winter or if spring will arrive early. This seemingly nonsensical holiday has pagan roots: as winter waned, our ancestors would look for signs of spring's arrival, such as animals reemerging from hibernation. For the Celts, their weather divination tactics followed the Cailleach, a winter crone goddess. If Imbolc brought sunshine, it meant that the goddess was out gathering firewood to prepare for the rest of winter. If the skies were gray, the Cailleach was asleep in her bed, for spring was near and she hadn't any need for additional kindling.

Practice Love Spells Responsibly

Love spells can be controversial: you never want to perform magic on someone without their consent. If you try to influence them to do something they'd otherwise not do, it could end poorly for both parties. I prefer to use love spells to strengthen a preexisting relationship, with either myself, a friend, or a romantic partner.

As you drink the potion, envision your heart opening with each sip. Imagine the libation filling your body, increasing your ability to give and receive love. If you're drinking with your lover or lovers, imagine their heart drawing toward yours, until they meet in a red, rosy glow. When you finish the drink, say:

"I am now ready to give and receive love. So mote it be."

Love Potion

MAKES 1 COCKTAIL

This Love Potion's potency comes from the syrup; it's infused with vanilla, cardamom, and rose water, which are all ruled by Venus, the planet of love. Sugar attracts with sweetness, honey energizes your spell with the sun's radiance, and black salt amplifies the flavors and protects against heartbreak. Make yourself a morning latte with the syrup to cultivate self-love, or mix it into the Love Potion cocktail to attract a romantic partner.

FOR THE SYRUP
(makes about 1 cup / 240ml)

2 tablespoons cardamom pods

1 cup (200 g) granulated sugar, scant

2 tablespoons honey

½ teaspoon rose water

½ teaspoon vanilla

Pinch of black salt

FOR THE LOVE POTION

1½ ounces gin

¾ ounce Love Potion Syrup

1 teaspoon freshly squeezed lime juice

3 to 4 ounces (90 to 120 ml) seltzer

Pinch of dried culinary rose petals, to garnish

1 lime wedge, to garnish

Make the syrup: Pour 1 cup (240 ml) water into a saucepan and bring to a simmer.

Add the cardamom pods to a mortar and lightly pound with a pestle until the seeds fall out of the pods. Stir the pods and seeds into the water, calling in the energy of Venus and thanking her for blessing the potion. Simmer for 10 minutes.

Add the sugar and stir clockwise as you visualize loving energy infusing into the syrup. Make sure the sugar fully dissolves.

Turn off the heat and let cool for 5 minutes. Add the honey and stir clockwise, imagining the sun infusing your potion with radiance. Add the rose water, vanilla, and salt. Stir clockwise, calling in the love you wish to attract.

Let cool for 5 minutes and strain. Store in an airtight container in the fridge for up to 2 weeks..

Make the cocktail: Add the gin, syrup, and lime juice to a glass and fill with ice. Stir clockwise for 30 seconds. Add the rose petals, pour in the seltzer, and stir to combine. Garnish with the lime wedge and serve.

Sleep Potion

MAKES 1 DRINK

Drink this sleep potion before bed to call in a peaceful night's rest. Chamomile has a magical ability to invite sweet dreams and soothe the mind, body, and spirit. Lavender has relaxing powers and wards off nightmares, all amplified by a pinch of cinnamon and protective black salt. Honey promotes healing, especially when charged in the moonlight, and the milk offers the nostalgia of our first food source. Everything comes together in a nurturing brew that will lull you into a deep sleep.
Pair with the Sweet Dreams Plate on page 78.

FOR THE MOON HONEY

1 jar of honey

FOR THE SLEEP POTION

2 teaspoons dried chamomile flowers

1 teaspoon dried lavender, plus more for serving

2 ounces (60 ml) milk

2 teaspoons Moon Honey

⅛ teaspoon cinnamon, plus more for serving

Pinch of black salt

Make the honey: Place the jar of honey in the light of a full or waning moon and let it charge overnight. Set aside 2 teaspoons for the potion. Store the remaining moon honey in a cool, dark place and use anytime you need a little extra rest.

Make the potion: Bring water to a boil in a kettle. Prepare a mug by pouring hot tap water into it and letting it sit.

Spoon the chamomile and lavender into a tea bag or strainer.

Empty your mug and pour 8 ounces (240 ml) of boiling water into it. Add the tea bag, cover, and let steep for 10 to 13 minutes.

Microwave the milk in 15-second intervals until warm.

Remove the tea bag and use a spoon to squeeze out the potent brew. Pour in the milk and stir, letting the aromas wash over you. Add the honey, cinnamon, and black salt. Stir clockwise, visualizing yourself drifting off into a deep sleep.

Serve with a dusting of cinnamon and a pinch of lavender.

Ritual Guidance

As you drink the potion, imagine a cool purple cloud washing over you, softening your muscles and slowing your thoughts. Feel your eyelids become heavy and your breathing slow to an even rhythm. Say, "I am now ready to rest deeply." Complete your bedtime rituals and let yourself drift away.

ORANGES

are a seasonal palate
cleanser and infuse the
plate with warmth
and vitality.

SAGE

promotes
longevity.

HONEY

balances the salty
cheeses and symbolizes
the promise of spring.

PEPITAS

bring salty crunch and
signal the time to plant
seeds for future harvests.

1 Roquefort

is creamy and rich with traces of
crunchy crystals and a piquant
burn, like a shot of good gin. Pair
with dried apricots and honey.

2 Brûléed feta

Brûléed feta tastes divine when
smeared onto shortbread cookies.
I recommend a 100% sheep's
milk feta, which has a richer
flavor and texture. Blend 3
ounces of feta with a couple
teaspoons of honey until
smooth, then scrape it into a
heatproof container. Sprinkle
with granulated sugar, and use
a brûlée torch to caramelize the
top until a browned crust forms.

3 Ossau Iraty comes

from southwest France, right by
the Spanish border. She's a hearty
mountain cheese with a firm,
buttery texture that melts in your
mouth with notes of almonds and
butterscotch. Pair with blackberry
preserves and pepitas.

BLACKBERRY
PRESERVES

pair with all the cheeses,
and blackberries are the sacred
food of Brigid, the Celtic
goddess of Imbolc.

LAVENDER

brings a calming,
healing energy.

SHORTBREAD COOKIES are rich with butter, an important ritual food for Imbolc feasts.

2

THE IMBOLC PLATE

This all-sheep's-milk platter celebrates the hope and stillness that Imbolc brings. For our ancestors, this cross-quarter fire festival meant survival. The harshest days of winter were behind them, and their resources were replenishing with the arrival of lambing season. This plate honors the start of the ewe's lactation cycle and the return of sunlight, especially with the brûléed feta. Pair with the Love Potion (page 71), amber ale, or Earl Grey tea.

3

APRICOTS bring a warm orange hue and represent the waxing sun.

THE LOVE SPELL PLATE

With all the kitsch of Valentine's Day, February is the perfect time for love spells, and a cheese plate makes for an alluring medium. Build this plate to seduce a lover or strengthen an established bond. Start by buying a big heart-shaped box filled with your favorite chocolates, then empty it out and line it with parchment or waxed paper. Set your intention for what kind of love spell you'd like to cast, then craft the platter inside the heart. Serve to your beloved alongside roses, candles, and champagne, or boost the potency of your spell with the Love Potion on page 71.

1 Triple-cream Brie

is one of the most luxurious cheeses out there. Dip a strawberry directly into the luscious center and drizzle with honey. Look for a small-format mini wheel such as Brillat-Savarin, Saint André (featured), or Kunik from Nettle Meadow Farm in New York.

ROSEMARY
brings protection against heartbreak.

HONEY
attracts love with sweetness and helps the love spell stick.

CHOCOLATE WAFERS
add a crunchy vehicle for the triple cream and pair with the marmalade and strawberries.

ALMONDS
symbolize fertility and possess aphrodisiac qualities.

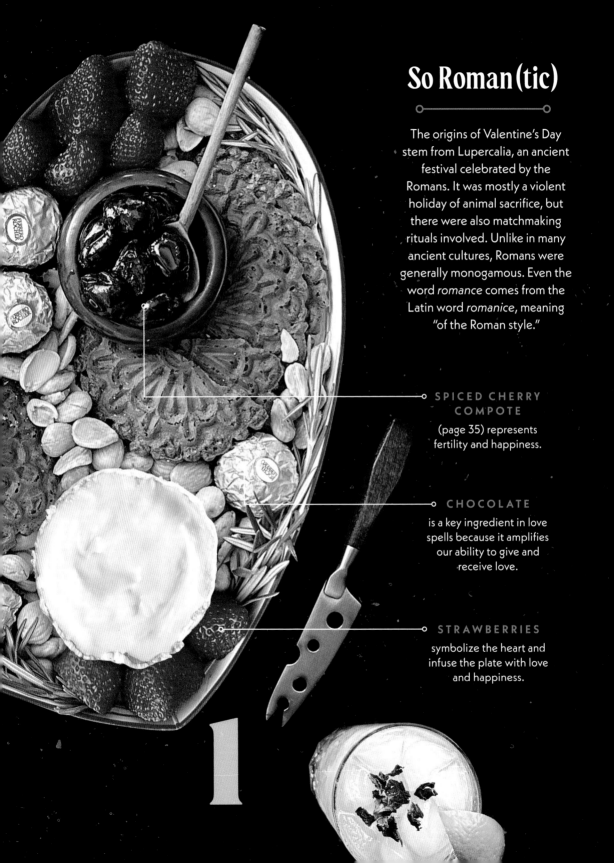

So Roman (tic)

The origins of Valentine's Day stem from Lupercalia, an ancient festival celebrated by the Romans. It was mostly a violent holiday of animal sacrifice, but there were also matchmaking rituals involved. Unlike in many ancient cultures, Romans were generally monogamous. Even the word *romance* comes from the Latin word *romanice*, meaning "of the Roman style."

SPICED CHERRY COMPOTE

(page 35) represents fertility and happiness.

CHOCOLATE

is a key ingredient in love spells because it amplifies our ability to give and receive love.

STRAWBERRIES

symbolize the heart and infuse the plate with love and happiness.

1

BLUEBERRY PRESERVES
are antioxidant-rich, instill
tranquility, and offer protection
in the dream state.

GRAPES
bring moon energy and
are believed to incite
lucid dreaming.

1 Midnight Moon

is a bright white goat Gouda
that's cloaked in black wax,
giving the appearance of the
moon in the sky. Whereas fresh
chèvre holds a signature tang,
goat's milk Gouda is remarkably
sweet, tasting of strawberries
in cream and brown butter.
The sugary, fruity notes are an
ideal pairing for grapes.

2 Soft-ripened goat's milk cheeses

are round and aglow with their
own luminescence, offering a
soft, fudgy texture and tangy
flavor that offsets the blueberry
preserves. Get a small wheel,
no more than 5 ounces, to
represent the full moon. I
recommend the ash-ripened
Bonne Bouche from Vermont
Creamery (pictured). Pair with
blueberry preserves.

LAVENDER
brings a relaxing
aroma that calms the
mind and body.

LAHVOSH STAR CRACKERS symbolize celestial energy.

THE SWEET DREAMS PLATE

While the nights stretch longer than the days, this period of deep winter reminds us to rest as nature hibernates around us. This plate is designed to induce a peaceful night of luxurious sleep and sweet dreams. Cheese itself has a natural ability to make us feel relaxed. The casein proteins break down into peptides and deliver a rush of dopamine, the "feel-good" hormone. Some believe that cheese can bring vivid dreams due to the amino acid tryptophan, which suggests that sweet dreams really are made of cheese. Pair with the Sleep Potion (page 72) or your nightcap of preference.

2

PISTACHIOS are high in magnesium, which helps lull you into a deep sleep.

OSTARA

Falling on the vernal equinox, Ostara marks the official end of winter. It's a celebration of new life as the earth awakens out of its deep slumber and green sprouts spring from its surface. While powerful fertile energy beckons the return of life, our planet is at an equilibrium: both day and night rule equally on this day. Though the scales are tipping into the kingdom of the sun, the shadow realm remains; for it is only in darkness that light may rule. The themes of rebirth and renewal are potent, with Easter, Passover, and Nowruz falling at this time. Look for the signs of spring's triumph over winter, such as daffodils, tree buds, animals, and other stirrings of life.

On or around September 20
Southern Hemisphere

Lemon Poppy Seed Goat Cheese Scones

MAKES 6 SCONES

These buttery scones are laced with pockets of goat cheese and drizzled with a lemon-spiked glaze. Lemon zest brings warm, blissful energies while also teasing out the chèvre's tangy notes. Poppy seeds are a symbol of fertility, echoing the vernal themes of virility. You don't have to be a good baker to make a good scone. It's all about using extra cold butter, not overmixing the dough, and adding a little Greek yogurt to make them melt-in-your-mouth moist. Pair with Black Pepper Orange Marmalade (page 66) and coffee or Earl Grey tea.

FOR THE SCONES

½ cup (115 g) unsalted butter, chilled

4 ounces (115 g) goat cheese, chilled

2 cups (240 g) flour

2 tablespoons poppy seeds

1 teaspoon baking powder

1 teaspoon Diamond Crystal kosher salt

½ teaspoon baking soda

½ cup (100 g) granulated sugar

1 tablespoon lemon zest (from about 2 lemons)

1 large egg

½ cup (120 ml) full-fat Greek yogurt

3 tablespoons freshly squeezed lemon juice (about 1½ lemons)

1 teaspoon vanilla extract

Position a rack in the upper third of the oven. Preheat the oven to 375°F (190°C).

Line a baking sheet with parchment paper or a silicone mat. Set aside.

Make the scones: Cut the butter into pea-sized pieces and crumble the goat cheese into nickel-size blobs. Keep both chilled in the fridge until you're ready to use them.

In the bowl of a food processor, pulse together the flour, poppy seeds, baking powder, salt, and baking soda.

In a separate bowl, combine the sugar and lemon zest. Gently massage them together to release the scent and infuse the sugar.

Add the lemon sugar to the dry ingredients in the food processor and pulse to combine.

(continued page 84)

Notes

- You can prepare the dough the day before. Just wrap it tightly in plastic wrap and chill in the fridge until you're ready to bake them.

- The scones also keep well in the freezer. Wrap the unglazed scones in a freezer bag and reheat them in the oven until they're warm and crisp on the outside, then drizzle with the glaze before serving.

FOR THE GLAZE

3 tablespoons confectioners' sugar

1½ teaspoons freshly squeezed lemon juice

Take the butter out of the fridge and add it to the food processor. Pulse a few times, just until the mixture looks like a coarse meal. Scrape the mixture into a large mixing bowl.

In a separate bowl, whisk together the egg, yogurt, lemon juice, and vanilla.

Pour the wet ingredients into the dry ingredients and gently mix until they're about 80 percent combined. Do not overmix.

Add the goat cheese to the mixture. Stir two or three more times, just to distribute the goat cheese. The dough will look pretty shaggy at this point, and that's a good thing.

Gently form the dough into a ball, and pat it into an 8-inch (20-cm) circle. Cut into six wedges, and transfer to the baking sheet.

Bake for about 20 minutes, or until lightly browned. The actual bake time will depend on your oven, so check the scones at 16 minutes and go from there.

Transfer to a wire rack to cool for about an hour.

Meanwhile, make the glaze: Sift the confectioners' sugar, and whisk in the lemon juice until smooth.

Drizzle the glaze over the scones and let it set for about 30 minutes before serving. Enjoy!

Ostara, the Dawn Goddess

The festival of Ostara is named for the Germanic goddess of the same name. Historic records of her origin are scarce, but many scholars believe she is the predecessor to Eostre, the Anglo-Saxon spring goddess for whom Easter is named. Others believe she is more closely related to Freya, the Nordic goddess of beauty, love, and resurrection. Regardless of Ostara's origins, today she is celebrated as a light-bringer, blessing the world with joy and new life.

Ritual Manifestation

As a symbol of fertility, eggs are an excellent medium for manifesting. As you steam, peel, and devil, whisper an invocation of whatever it is you wish to bring to harvest. Ask the egg to fertilize the soil of your intention.

Blue Cheese Deviled Eggs

MAKES 2 DOZEN DEVILS

Eggs are perhaps the quintessential food of Ostara because they represent new life. As spring breaks through winter's shell, nature seems to hatch all around us. Even the yolks themselves are symbols of the sun. I love the ritual of making deviled eggs: cooking them until their insides solidify, peeling away their shells, and gently removing the yolks so I can mash them with fats and flavorings before returning them to their silky white beds. I recommend steaming the eggs rather than boiling them, which makes them easier to peel. The secret to perfect deviled eggs is butter and mayo, a trick I learned from Julia Child's recipe. My version is spiked with fiery horseradish, chives, paprika, and creamy blue cheese, which add a special piquancy. That extra heat is essential because the "devil" refers to the spicy flavors, which are evocative of hellfire. Serve on the Ostara Brunch Plate (page 108) or the Afternoon Tea Plate (page 110).

1 dozen large eggs

½ cup (115 g) mayo, at room temperature

2 tablespoons unsalted butter, at room temperature

2 teaspoons horseradish

2 tablespoons chives chopped, plus an extra teaspoon for garnish

3 ounces (85 g) creamy blue cheese, plus an extra ounce for garnish

Kosher salt and freshly ground black pepper

Paprika, to garnish

Steam the eggs: Fill a pot with enough water to reach the bottom of a steam basket. Place the basket inside the pot and bring the water to a boil.

Place the eggs in a single layer at the bottom of the basket. Set a timer for 15 minutes. While the eggs are cooking, set up an ice bath: fill a large bowl halfway with ice and then fill the rest of the bowl with cold water.

Once the eggs are cooked, transfer them to the ice bath and let chill for 10 minutes.

Carefully peel the eggs, then cut each in half. Scoop the yolks into a medium mixing bowl and set the whites aside.

To the bowl with the yolks, add the mayo, butter, horseradish, and chives and mash with a fork until smooth.

(continued on page 88)

BLUE CHEESE DEVILED EGGS, *continued*

Crumble the blue cheese into a small bowl, and microwave at 5-second intervals until the cheese is softened. Let cool for a minute.

Add the blue cheese to the yolk mixture and continue mashing until smooth. Taste and season with the salt and pepper.

Scoop the yolk mixture into a pastry bag or plastic bag, and cut a ¼ inch off of the corner.

Sprinkle the egg whites with a pinch of salt. Fill with the yolk mixture just before serving.

Garnish with a sprinkle of paprika, chives, and a touch of crumbled blue cheese.

Easter Bunnies

The Easter bunny and his colorful eggs come from the folklore of Ostara. One day, the spring goddess came upon an injured bird lying in the snow. She brought the bird back to life by transforming it into a white hare with the power to lay beautiful eggs during the early days of spring. The swift hare assumed the role of her messenger, delivering the eggs to all who worshiped Ostara during the vernal equinox.

New Potato Salad

SERVES 4 TO 6

One of the most beautiful characteristics of the blessed potato is its year-round versatility, but there's something peculiarly novel about the new potatoes of springtime. Tender, petite, and covered with a delicate skin, baby reds are perfect for potato salads. I love how this salad encapsulates the themes of Ostara by balancing the grounding earth energy of potatoes with the fiery powers of horseradish, dill, scallions, and mustard, finished with a generous shower of aged cow's milk cheese infused with the energy of a sun-kissed summer pasture. I used an extra aged wedge of Gruyère Alpage from Switzerland, but I also recommend Pleasant Ridge Reserve from Wisconsin. If you can't find a summer milk cheese, you can use a bandaged cheddar or even Mimolette. Serve this bright and satisfying New Potato Salad alongside the Brie and Ham Sandwich (page 93).

2 tablespoons Diamond Crystal kosher salt, plus more for seasoning

1½ pounds (685 g) new potatoes, washed

½ cup Lemon Dill Dressing (opposite page)

3 scallions, dark green parts removed and thinly sliced

2 tablespoons roughly chopped dill, plus more for garnish

½ teaspoon freshly ground black pepper, plus more for seasoning

Flaky salt

Freshly squeezed lemon juice

3 ounces (85 g) Gruyère Alpage cow's milk cheese

Fill a 4-quart pot with water and add the salt. Bring to a boil. Add the potatoes and cook until fork-tender, about 8 to 10 minutes. Drain and let cool.

When the potatoes are cool enough to handle, cut them into quarters. Add to a large mixing bowl.

Pour the dressing over the potatoes. Toss to combine.

Add the scallions, 2 tablespoons of dill, and ½ teaspoon black pepper. Toss to combine.

Taste for seasoning and add salt, pepper, and lemon juice as needed.

Using a microplane or the smallest holes on a box grater, finely shred half of the cheese over the potato salad. Toss to combine.

Transfer the salad to a serving dish and grate the rest of the cheese over the salad. Finish with additional black pepper, salt, lemon juice, and dill.

Lemon Dill Dressing

1 teaspoon horseradish

1 teaspoon whole-grain mustard

2 tablespoons freshly squeezed
    lemon juice (from about
    1 small lemon)

Pinch of kosher salt

6 tablespoons extra-virgin
    olive oil

1 ½ tablespoons dill, chopped

In a small bowl, whisk together the horseradish and mustard. Whisk in the lemon juice and salt.

Slowly drizzle in the olive oil, whisking continuously until the dressing is emulsified. Whisk in the dill and set aside.

Note

A traditional jambon-beurre
has the ham against the butter,
which is how I built the
sandwich for this recipe.
However, the sandwich is also
excellent when you put the
radishes against the butter and
the ham against the mustard.
Try it both ways and see
which you prefer!

Brie and Ham Sandwich

MAKES 1 SANDWICH

Ham has been traditional springtime fare for millennia. Historically, pigs were slaughtered in autumn, and the meat was salted and cured throughout the winter. When spring arrived, the ham was ready to enjoy during celebratory feasts such as Ostara or, later, Easter. The preserved meat is symbolic of our endurance through the bitter winter. This sandwich is itself a celebration of vernal flavors, especially with the lemony dill compound butter and crisp radishes. I recommend using a Brie with a little funk, such as Brie de Meaux or Brie Fermier. Honey-baked Easter ham is my preferred meat here, but a little prosciutto will do just fine as well. Serve with the Spring Tea (page 105) or a crisp saison or other wheat beer.

1 demi baguette, or about half of a full baguette

1½ ounces (40 g) Brie

2 small radishes, trimmed, washed, dried, and thinly sliced

1½ tablespoons Lemon Dill Compound Butter (page 102)

2 ounces (55 g) French ham (about 2 slices)

Freshly ground black pepper

1½ teaspoons Dijon mustard

Cut the baguette in half lengthwise.

Thinly slice the Brie lengthwise, leaving an even rind-to-paste ratio.

Spread the Lemon Dill Compound Butter onto the bottom of the baguette. Layer the ham on top of the butter.

Evenly layer the cheese over the ham and follow with the radish slices and a sprinkle of black pepper.

Swipe the top of the baguette with the mustard. Close the sandwiches. Slice in half and serve.

Lavender Goat Cheese Truffles

MAKES 12 TO 16 TRUFFLES

As elegant and indulgent as ganache-filled chocolates, these goat cheese truffles require just a little more skill than it takes to make a cheese ball. A kiss of lavender teases out the floral notes in the goat cheese, while infusing the truffles with loving, protecting energies. The milk chocolate brings its own romantic powers while complementing the earthiness of the chèvre and contrasting against the tart and tangy notes. Serve the truffles on the Afternoon Tea Plate (page 110) and pair with the Spring Tea (page 105).

6 ounces (170 g) fresh goat cheese, at room temperature

1 teaspoon ground culinary-grade dried lavender, plus more for garnish

2 teaspoons honey

1 tablespoon confectioners' sugar

½ teaspoon Diamond Crystal kosher salt

10 ounces (460 g) milk chocolate, finely chopped (see note on page 96)

In a medium mixing bowl, beat together the goat cheese and half of the ground lavender using an electric mixer. The amount of lavender you'll need varies depending on its freshness, so add ¼ teaspoon at a time and taste as you go. When you're happy with the floral flavor, add the honey, confectioners' sugar, and salt and beat until thoroughly combined.

Cover and let chill in the fridge until firm, about 30 minutes. Line a baking sheet with parchment paper.

Scoop the cheese mixture with a melon baller or a teaspoon and roll in your hands to make evenly sized balls.

Place onto the baking sheet lined with parchment paper. Chill in the fridge until firm, about 30 more minutes.

Pour three quarters of the chocolate into a heatproof glass bowl and microwave for 20 seconds. Stir well with a rubber spatula, and microwave another 20 seconds. Stir again, then microwave for an additional 20 seconds.

(continued on page 96)

If there are any unmelted pieces of chocolate at this point, microwave for another 10 seconds, then stir until smooth. Add in the remaining chocolate, and stir until completely smooth.

Use two spoons to lower a truffle into the melted chocolate, twirl it until it's coated, and place it back on the parchment paper. Repeat with all the truffles.

Sprinkle with the reserved lavender and let sit at room temperature until the chocolate shells are hard.

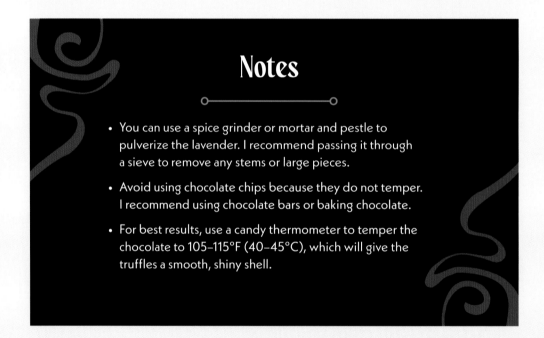

Notes

- You can use a spice grinder or mortar and pestle to pulverize the lavender. I recommend passing it through a sieve to remove any stems or large pieces.

- Avoid using chocolate chips because they do not temper. I recommend using chocolate bars or baking chocolate.

- For best results, use a candy thermometer to temper the chocolate to 105–115°F (40–45°C), which will give the truffles a smooth, shiny shell.

Fresh Goat Cheese

Fresh chèvre is the quintessential cheese of springtime because that's when the goats are out feasting on the lush new pastures and giving birth to their babies. This kick-starts their lactation cycle, and the cheeses made from these early batches of milk glow with the vibrancy of spring. Though fresh goat cheese is made all over the world, it's known as chèvre because it's the French who made it so popular. The name directly translates as "goat" and can refer to a variety of goat's milk cheeses but is most commonly associated with the bright, cloudlike fresh variety.

Sesame Cream Crackers

MAKES ABOUT 40 CRACKERS

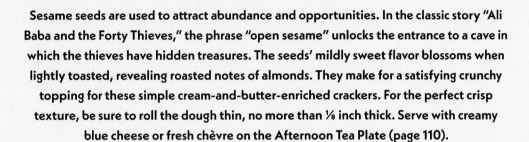

Sesame seeds are used to attract abundance and opportunities. In the classic story "Ali Baba and the Forty Thieves," the phrase "open sesame" unlocks the entrance to a cave in which the thieves have hidden treasures. The seeds' mildly sweet flavor blossoms when lightly toasted, revealing roasted notes of almonds. They make for a satisfying crunchy topping for these simple cream-and-butter-enriched crackers. For the perfect crisp texture, be sure to roll the dough thin, no more than ⅛ inch thick. Serve with creamy blue cheese or fresh chèvre on the Afternoon Tea Plate (page 110).

2 teaspoons white sesame seeds

1 cup (120 g) all-purpose flour, plus more for rolling out the dough

½ teaspoon Diamond Crystal kosher salt

3 tablespoons unsalted butter, cut into pats

¼ cup (60 ml) heavy whipping cream

2 tablespoons water, plus more for brushing

¾ teaspoon freshly ground black pepper

½ teaspoon flaky salt

Preheat the oven to 350°F (175°C). Line a baking sheet with parchment paper or a silicone mat.

Place the sesame seeds on the baking sheet and toast in the oven for about 4 minutes. Stir them around, then return to the oven and toast until golden and nutty, about 8 minutes. Let cool for 5 minutes, then transfer to a bowl.

To the bowl of a food processor, add the flour and salt and pulse to combine. Add the butter and pulse until incorporated.

Mix the cream with 2 tablespoons of water, then pour in while running the processor until the dough fully comes together. If it's too dry, add more water a teaspoon at a time until the dough holds together without being sticky. Form into a ball and gently knead for about a minute until smooth.

(continued on page 100)

SESAME CREAM CRACKERS, *continued*

Dust your work surface with flour and roll out the dough until it's no more than an ⅛ inch (3 mm) thick. The thinner the dough, the crisper the crackers will be.

Transfer to the baking sheet. Use a butter knife to gently score the dough into squares, roughly 2 x 2 inches (5 x 5 cm).

Using a pastry brush, lightly brush the crackers with water. Then sprinkle with the toasted sesame seeds, black pepper, and salt.

Bake until golden brown, about 16 to 18 minutes. Let cool completely, then break apart along the scored lines.

Store in an airtight container at room temperature for up to 5 days.

Lemon Dill Compound Butter

MAKES ½ CUP (115 G)

This simple compound butter is infused with fresh dill, one of my favorite springtime flavors. Dill has the power to dispel negative energies and balance both your emotional and mental selves, especially when combined with uplifting and purifying lemon. Serve with funky blue cheese and crackers or spread onto the Brie and Ham Sandwich (page 93).

½ cup (115 g) unsalted butter, softened

1 tablespoon lemon zest (about 1 lemon)

½ teaspoon freshly squeezed lemon juice

2 tablespoons washed, dried, and chopped fresh dill

¼ teaspoon freshly ground black pepper

¼ teaspoon flaky salt, plus more to taste

Add the butter to a bowl and spread it around until it evenly coats the bottom. Sprinkle in the lemon zest and juice, dill, and pepper. Use a fork to mash it up until fully combined. Gently fold in ¼ teaspoon of salt. Taste for seasoning and add more if needed.

You can store the butter immediately, or if you're making it ahead of time, transfer it to waxed paper and roll it into a log. Wrap it up in the waxed paper and store it in a sealed plastic bag. It will keep in the fridge for about 10 days and in the freezer for 6 months.

Thyme Lemon Curd

MAKES ABOUT ¾ CUP (150 G)

This curd is infused with fresh thyme, a powerful herb beloved for its optimistic energies, making it a popular ingredient in spells for courage, happiness, beauty, and healing. It has a woodsy floral note that pairs well with bright, sunny lemons, especially their aromatic zest. Rubbing the sugar together with the thyme and lemon zest unveils their aromatic oils, perfuming the resulting curd with deep, complex flavors. Serve with soft-ripened goat cheese and Spring Tea (page 105) or on the Ostara Brunch Plate (page 108).

⅓ cup (70 g) granulated sugar

1 tablespoon fresh thyme leaves

½ tablespoon lemon zest (about 1 lemon)

¼ cup (60 ml) freshly squeezed lemon juice (about 2 lemons)

1 large egg

1 large egg yolk

½ teaspoon Diamond Crystal kosher salt

3½ tablespoons cold unsalted butter, cubed

In a heatproof bowl, combine the sugar, thyme, and lemon zest, massaging the ingredients together with your fingers until sandy and fragrant. Envision the waxing sunlight filling your home with optimistic, hopeful energies.

Whisk in the lemon juice, egg, egg yolk, and salt.

Fill a saucepan with a few inches of water and bring to a simmer. Set the heatproof bowl on top.

Cook, whisking constantly, until the mixture thickens, about 7 to 9 minutes.

Remove from the heat, and whisk in the butter until it's fully melted and the mixture is silky smooth.

Set a fine-mesh sieve over a bowl and pour the mixture through. Discard the solids, and place a piece of plastic wrap directly onto the surface of the curd. Transfer to the fridge and chill until cold, about 1½ hours.

Store in an airtight container in the fridge. It will keep for about a week.

Lemon curd is one of my favorite accompaniments for spring cheese plates. The tart flavors tease out the tang in soft chèvres and brighten the herbaceous, floral notes in Alpine-style cheeses. I love how the silky, rich texture nestles into a soft pillow of ricotta or beds a slice of oozing triple cream Brie.

Spring Tea

MAKES 24 OUNCES AND SERVES 4

This simple tea awakens the senses from their wintery slumber. The bright, floral flavors celebrate light's triumph over darkness with the loving, passionate powers of roses, purifying lemon, confidence-invoking jasmine, and grassy, revitalizing green tea. Rose hips promote peaceful, balanced energies and are rich in vitamin C, which strengthens the immune system and boosts collagen production. Strawberries are potent symbols not only of love but also of overcoming barriers like the long, dark winter. Serve with honey and lemon to boost the flavors and solar energies of the tea. The bright, verdant flavors are an excellent match with chèvres of all ages. Pair with the Lemon Poppy Seed Goat Cheese Scones (page 82) and the Afternoon Tea Plate (page 110).

¼ cup (30 g) rose hips

1 tablespoon rose petals

Two 1 x 3-inch (2.5 cm x 7.5 cm) strips lemon peel

2 strawberries, stems removed and sliced

2 jasmine green tea bags

Honey and lemon wedges, to serve

Fill a kettle with water and bring to a boil.

Combine the rose hips and petals in tea bags or a strainer. Set aside.

Place the lemon peel inside a teapot and add the sliced strawberries. Pour 24 ounces of boiling water over.

Add the rose tea bags or strainer and let steep for 9 minutes. Add the jasmine green tea bags and let steep for 4 more minutes.

Pour into teacups and serve with the honey and lemon wedges.

As you drink the tea, envision all you wish to bring to fruition sprouting out of the soft, brown earth in bright green shoots. Envision a flower bud forming and opening with each sip. When you finish the tea, speak an incantation that matches your intention.

Compost the tea bags or bury them in the earth to complete your ritual.

Garlic Bloody Mary

MAKES 1 COCKTAIL

Savory, potent garlic has powerful protective energies and is often used to prevent illness, ward off the evil eye, and quicken the desired effect of any spell. Its natural antifungal and antibacterial properties can reduce plaque buildup in your arteries, regulate blood sugar, and lower your blood pressure. It's about as beneficial for your blood as it is delicious in this Bloody Mary. Here, garlic and a little dill are infused straight into vodka much like a tincture, which is a potion of herbs or other medicinals steeped in alcohol. The infused vodka brings a powerful savory flavor to this Garlic Bloody Mary. Enjoy with dill Havarti, aged cheddar, or on the Ostara Brunch Plate (page 108).

FOR THE GARLIC-INFUSED VODKA (makes 2 cups / 465 ml)

2 cups (475 ml) vodka

3 to 4 garlic cloves, peeled and smashed

2 dill sprigs, about 3 inches (7.6 cm) long

FOR THE GARLIC BLOODY MARY

¾ cup (180 ml) tomato juice

1½ ounces garlic-infused vodka

1 teaspoon Worcestershire sauce

1 dash hot sauce

Freshly ground black pepper

1 teaspoon celery salt

1 teaspoon kosher salt

Celery stalk, lemon wedge, and 1 skewer with cubes of white cheddar, cornichons, and thinly sliced salami, for garnish

Make the infused vodka: Add the vodka, garlic, and dill to a clean glass jar. Steep for 48 hours, then strain. Store in an airtight container in the fridge or freezer for about 2 months.

Make the cocktail: Fill a mixing glass with lots of ice. Add the tomato juice, vodka, Worcestershire, hot sauce, and a healthy pinch of black pepper. Stir for about 30 seconds.

Mix the celery salt and kosher salt together and spread out onto a small plate. Use the lemon wedge to wet the rim of a tall glass. Dip the rim into the salt and roll it around a bit until it's coated.

Fill the rimmed glass with ice and strain the Bloody Mary over the ice.

Garnish with the celery , lemon wedge, and skewer and serve.

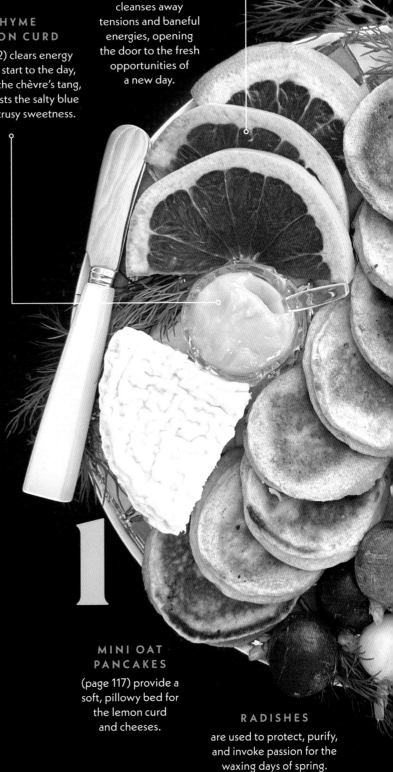

THYME LEMON CURD

(page 102) clears energy for a fresh start to the day, teases out the chèvre's tang, and contrasts the salty blue with its citrusy sweetness.

GRAPEFRUIT

cleanses away tensions and baneful energies, opening the door to the fresh opportunities of a new day.

1 Soft-ripened goat cheese

is at her peak during the spring, especially since the bright, tangy flavors pair so seamlessly with the fresh flavors of the vernal equinox. Look for delicate, small-format wheels like French Chabichou, Bijou from Vermont Creamery, or the paprika-infused Piper's Pyramide from Capriole Goat Cheese in Indiana. Pair with the lemon curd on a pancake.

2 Buttermilk Blue

has a creamy texture and salty tang that complements the smoky bacon and bitter notes in black coffee. If you can't find a buttermilk blue, look for something with a similarly soft texture, like Oregon Blue from Rogue Creamery, Cashel Blue from Ireland, or Saint Agur from France. Whichever cheese you choose, I recommend using the same one in the deviled eggs for a truly perfect pairing.

MINI OAT PANCAKES

(page 117) provide a soft, pillowy bed for the lemon curd and cheeses.

RADISHES

are used to protect, purify, and invoke passion for the waxing days of spring.

DILL

represents balance, attracts wealth, and imbues the plate with protective energies.

2

THE OSTARA BRUNCH PLATE

Spring is a time for beginnings, so it makes sense to celebrate its arrival at the start of a new day with an abundant brunch plate. I love the indulgence of the belated morning meal, a lazy ritual best paired with a little hair of the dog and followed by a long nap. This platter features all of breakfast's best: crisp bacon, oat pancakes sweetened with lemon curd, fresh grapefruit, and Blue Cheese Deviled Eggs. Soft-ripened goat cheese brings a bright flavor and fudgy texture, while creamy blue adds a salty richness. Serve alongside a fresh batch of hot coffee and the Garlic Bloody Mary (page 106).

BACON

adds a satisfying crunch and a smoky flavor that complements the creamy blue cheese.

BLUE CHEESE DEVILED EGGS

(page 87) symbolize new beginnings, while the rich yellow yolks imbue the plate with solar energy.

SHORTBREAD
COOKIES

are a buttery, crisp
vehicle for the
chèvre and a
substitute for the
traditional scone.

RASPBERRY
ROSE JAM

complements the
chèvre's tang and
fulfills the teatime
ritual of dolloping.

THE
AFTER-NOON TEA PLATE

I have long been fascinated by the British ritual of afternoon tea: the delicate scones dolloped with jam and elegant finger sandwiches accompanied by a pot of hot tea. It's a ceremony of indulgence, a moment to luxuriate in fancy little snacks paired with a carefully brewed potion. This format is befitting for a springtime cheese platter. I deconstructed the savory sandwiches into a build-your-own concoction, and I substituted the traditional scone with clotted cream for shortbread cookies and fresh chèvre. Serve alongside the Lemon Poppy Seed Goat Cheese Scones (page 82) and a pot of Earl Grey or Spring Tea (page 105).

1

STRAWBERRIES

are a classic fruit served at afternoon tea and infuse the spread with a cheerful, uplifting energy.

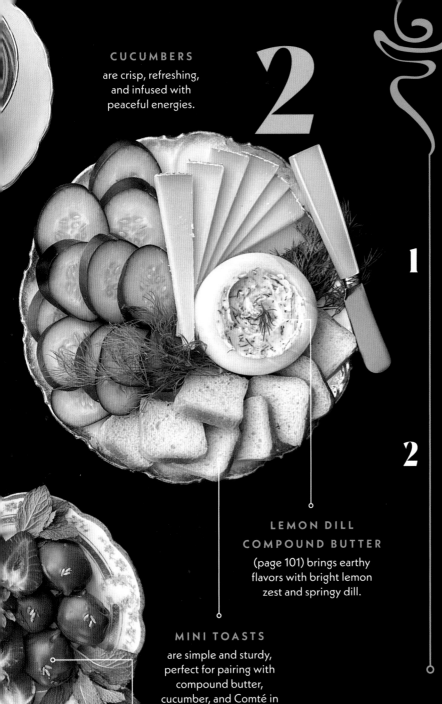

CUCUMBERS

are crisp, refreshing, and infused with peaceful energies.

2

1 Goat cheese

acts as a substitute for the traditional clotted cream. The quintessential cheese of spring, fresh chèvre is spreadable, tangy, and rich with delicate herbaceous notes that complement a variety of teas. Smear onto the shortbread cookies and top with raspberry rose jam.

2 Comté

is buttery, toothsome, and rich with grassy notes. My favorite wheels are made in the summertime when the cows are grazing on the Alpine pasture. Their diet of mountain flowers and herbs perfumes the cheese with a bouquet of vernal aromatics. Layer onto a well-buttered mini toast and finish with a slice of cucumber for makeshift tea sandwiches.

LEMON DILL COMPOUND BUTTER

(page 101) brings earthy flavors with bright lemon zest and springy dill.

MINI TOASTS

are simple and sturdy, perfect for pairing with compound butter, cucumber, and Comté in lieu of tea sandwiches.

LAVENDER GOAT CHEESE TRUFFLES

(page 94) add a sweet, floral little bite of indulgence.

1 Aries: Pecorino Pepato

The leaders of the zodiac are known for their fiery strength, lively passion, and powerful confidence. Aries are symbolized by the ram, so a peppercorn-infused sheep's milk cheese is the obvious choice.

2 Cancer: Burrata

Nurturing and intuitive, Cancers are ruled by their potent emotional force. They're softies, but you often have to break through their shell first, much like a ball of burrata.

3 Libra: Dunbarton Blue

This Venus-ruled air sign is dedicated to beauty and peacemaking. Represented by the scale, Libras strive for harmony much like this gorgeous Wisconsin cheese that strikes the balance between cheddar and blue.

4 Aquarius: a wrinkled, soft-ripened cheese

Aquarians are innovative, technical, and highly intellectual with a knack for self-expression. The cerebral wrinkles that cover soft-ripened cheeses like Apricity from Alemar in Minnesota represent this brainy air sign.

TAURUS: SESAME CREAM CRACKERS

Resourceful and generous, Taureans are known for their love of comfort and appreciation for epicurean delights. These salty crackers (page 99) are enriched with butter and cream to represent their symbol: the bull.

GEMINI: RHUBARB ROSE COMPOTE

Talkative, inquisitive Geminis are defined by their dual nature. This compote unites the masculine energies of tart rhubarb with feminine rosewater and sweet vanilla, representing the duplicity of the twin sign.

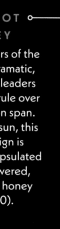

LEO: HOT HONEY

The performers of the zodiac are dramatic, natural-born leaders that yearn to rule over your attention span. Ruled by the sun, this fixed fire sign is perfectly encapsulated by solar-powered, chili-infused honey (page 130).

VIRGO: BAGUETTE

The perfectionists of the zodiac, Virgos are known for their dedication and rigor. A baguette might seem simple, but the technique can take years to perfect and requires the proficient expertise of this mutable earth sign.

PISCES: BOQUERONES

Represented by two fish swimming in opposite directions, this mutable water sign is often torn between their fantasies and reality. Briny and sweet, Spanish boquerones represents their gentle demeanors.

THE ZODIAC PLATE

The vernal equinox marks the start of the zodiac calendar. At the same moment as the spring equinox, the sun moves out of dreamy Pisces into fiery Aries and begins the astrological cycle. This platter celebrates the full spectrum of the zodiac, with each element representing a different sign.

4

SAGITTARIUS: BLACK PEPPER ORANGE MARMALADE

Confident and optimistic, Sagittarians live to uplift others with their infectious energy and are ruled by their wanderlust. Black Pepper Orange Marmalade (page 66) mirrors their sunny dispositions.

CAPRICORN: MARCONA ALMONDS

Symbolized by the mythic sea goat, these pragmatic overachievers love to make money as much as they love to spend it. Marcona almonds are the perfect expensive indulgence for these cardinal earth signs.

SCORPIO: DARK CHOCOLATE

Secretive and discerning, Scorpios are strategic, unafraid to call you out on your bullshit, and immovable in their resolutions. Dark chocolate is just as complex and enchanting, while also sharing their ruling planet: Mars.

3

BELTANE

The midpoint between the vernal equinox and the summer solstice, Beltane celebrates the high point of spring. Nature is surging with virility as the bees buzz among an abundance of colorful blossoms, and chirping birds forage for worms to bring back to their full nests. It's a festival of fertility and a portal to summer, as we inch our way toward the longest day of the year. The oldest holiday in Celtic mythology, Beltane is named for the Old Irish word meaning "bright fire" and was commonly celebrated by dancing around balefires for protection and health. Sitting directly opposite the wheel to Samhain, it is a time to cultivate and nurture all that you intend to bring to harvest this year.

Mini Oat Pancakes with Lemon Curd and Robiola

MAKES 30 MINI PANCAKES

Oatmeal cakes and breads are customary foods for the festival of Beltane. In Scotland, an oat-based, griddle-cooked flatbread called bannock was traditionally eaten on the morning of Beltane to ensure a healthful harvest. I've reinterpreted this ritual with these miniature pancakes designed for pairing with soft, creamy cheeses on breakfast platters. Like Scottish bannocks, they're made with oats, which are associated with luck and fertility. A little vanilla brings loving, nurturing energy and perfumes the batter with a sweet floral scent.

¾ cup (80 g) all-purpose flour

¾ cup (75 g) rolled oats

2 tablespoons granulated sugar

1 teaspoon baking powder

½ teaspoon Diamond Crystal kosher salt

1 cup (240 ml) whole milk

3 tablespoons unsalted butter

1 large egg

2 teaspoons vanilla extract

2 to 3 tablespoons salted butter, for cooking the pancakes

Thyme Lemon Curd (page 102), to serve

Robiola, goat cheese, or triple cream Brie, to serve

Add the flour, oats, sugar, baking powder, and salt to a blender and pulse until they're fully ground. Add the milk and pulse until incorporated. Let sit for 10 minutes.

Melt the unsalted butter in the microwave in 5-second increments. Let cool for about 5 minutes.

Add the cooled butter, egg, and vanilla to the blender. Blend until smooth, scraping the walls of the blender as needed.

Preheat your oven to the lowest setting. Heat a nonstick skillet or griddle over medium heat.

Add a pat of butter. When it starts to foam, use a tablespoon to ladle the batter onto the pan. Cook about six pancakes at a time, making sure they're evenly spaced on the pan.

(continued on page 118)

MINI OAT PANCAKES WITH LEMON CURD
AND ROBIOLA, *continued*

Cook until bubbles start to form on the surface of the cakes, about 2 minutes. Flip and cook for 2 more minutes. Flip again and cook until golden brown, another 2 minutes per side.

Transfer the pancakes to a baking sheet and keep warm in the oven.

Repeat until all the batter is used. Transfer the warm pancakes to a platter and serve dolloped with lemon curd and robiola, goat cheese, or triple cream Brie.

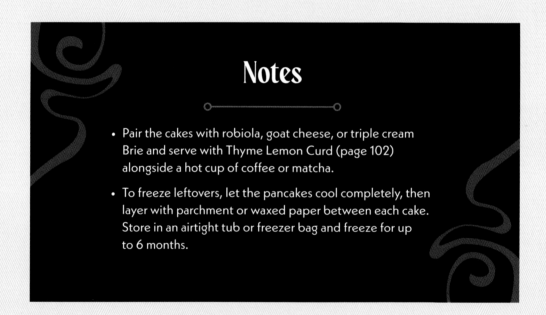

Notes

- Pair the cakes with robiola, goat cheese, or triple cream Brie and serve with Thyme Lemon Curd (page 102) alongside a hot cup of coffee or matcha.

- To freeze leftovers, let the pancakes cool completely, then layer with parchment or waxed paper between each cake. Store in an airtight tub or freezer bag and freeze for up to 6 months.

The Beltane Balefires

Beltane is one of the four Celtic fire festivals, along with Imbolc, Lughnasadh, and Samhain. In the case of Beltane, the fires were used to cultivate fertile energies and protect people and livestock from the pests, diseases, and evil spirits that threatened the upcoming harvests. On the night before the first of May, a day known as Walpurgisnacht in northern Europe, all fires were extinguished, and the land fell into total darkness. Germany deemed May Eve Hexennacht, meaning "witches' night," and celebrated this festival as much as you would Samhain: by dressing in costumes, playing pranks, and leaving offerings to appease the spirits. The new fires were built from sacred woods and started by rubbing sticks together. Livestock were driven through fires, while people jumped over flames. Coals from the balefires were brought home to light the hearth, and the remaining ashes were used in anointing rituals.

Notes

○────────────────○

- For a double batch, use a Dutch oven or another wide, heavy-bottom pot that has the surface area to properly brown the onions. You'll also need to increase the caramelization time by at least 10 minutes.

- If you're sensitive to onion cutting like I am, here are some old witches' tips: freeze the onions for 20 minutes before cutting, use an extra-sharp knife, and hold a match in your teeth as you slice. I don't fully understand why these rituals work, but they do.

- If you don't own a food processor, chop the feta as finely as possible, whisk it with the Greek yogurt until thoroughly combined, and continue with the recipe.

Triple-Onion Feta Dip

MAKES ABOUT 12 OUNCES (330 ML) AND SERVES 4 TO 6

This creamy dip starts with a base of whipped feta and yogurt, then is blessed with an ungodly amount of onion in the form of caramelized red onions, chopped fresh chives, and onion powder. Make sure to caramelize the hell out of those onions! That deep, sweet flavor is the backbone of this dip, so don't rush the process. Serve with potato chips, toasted pita, or cucumbers and bell peppers. Pair with a crisp lager, chilled rosé, or Smoky Hibiscus Paloma (page 132).

2 tablespoons extra-virgin olive oil, plus more for garnish

1 large red onion, thinly sliced into half-moons

Kosher salt

2 to 3 garlic cloves, minced

4 ounces (110 ml) Greek yogurt, full fat preferred

6 ounces feta (170 g) in brine, at room temperature

½ teaspoon onion powder

¼ teaspoon garlic powder

¼ teaspoon freshly ground black pepper, plus more to taste

Kosher salt

2 tablespoons chopped fresh chives, plus more for garnish

Lemon wedge, to finish

Flaky salt, to finish

Pour the olive oil into a large skillet or Dutch oven and heat over medium-low heat. Once the oil starts to shimmer, add the onions and a big pinch of kosher salt.

Cook for about 45 minutes, stirring regularly. Once the onions are nice and caramelized, add the garlic cloves and cook for 2 more minutes. Stir often to prevent burning.

Remove from heat and let cool for about 10 minutes. Once cool to the touch, roughly chop and set aside.

Scrape the Greek yogurt into the bowl of a food processor. Drain the feta, and crumble or chop. Add to the yogurt.

Pulse until whipped and smooth. Add the onion powder, garlic powder, and black pepper. Pulse until smooth, then taste and season with kosher salt and more black pepper. Pulse again to combine.

Transfer the mixture to a medium serving bowl and stir in the chives. If making ahead of time, cover and chill in the fridge for 3 to 5 days. Store the onions separately in an airtight container.

Create a shallow well in the center of the dip, and fill with the chopped onions. Finish with a squeeze of lemon, black pepper, flaky salt, and more chives. Serve immediately.

Grain Goddess Salad

MAKES 1 SALAD

This nourishing salad honors Demeter, the Greek goddess of grain and agriculture. Farro comes from wheat, and like other grains, it's associated with the elements of earth, abundance, and rebirth. Cooked until soft and chewy, its fertile energy is enhanced with chopped spears of pickled asparagus and salty roasted sunflower seeds. I also added crisp radish slices and fresh herbs, tossed with a lemony Greek goddess–inspired dressing, all crowned with thick shavings of a salty, flaky cow's milk cheese. Parmigiano-Reggiano is the obvious choice here, but I used Vella Dry Jack, a legendary California cheese born of Italian immigrants. Prepare the salad with visualization to plant the seeds for whatever it is you wish to bring to harvest, and thank the agricultural goddess for the blessings of sustenance. Pair with a lemony seltzer or a cup of Spring Tea (page 105).

1 cup (160 g) cooked farro, fully cooled

½ scallion, dark green parts removed and sliced

2 tablespoons roughly chopped fresh dill, divided

2 tablespoons roughly chopped fresh parsley leaves, divided

3 tablespoons Greek Goddess dressing (opposite page)

Pinch of flaky salt

Freshly ground black pepper

¼ cup (45 g) roughly chopped Pickled Asparagus (page 131)

1 medium radish, thinly sliced

½ ounce (14 g) Parmigiano-Reggiano, Vella Dry Jack, or other grana-style cheese

1 tablespoon roasted and salted sunflower seeds

In a medium mixing bowl, add the farro, scallion, 1 tablespoon of dill, and 1 tablespoon of parsley. Add the dressing and mix until fully coated. Sprinkle with the flaky salt and a couple cracks of black pepper. Toss again and taste a leaf for seasoning. Adjust as needed.

Add the asparagus and radishes. Using a vegetable peeler, shave most of the Parm or other cheese onto the salad. Gently toss a couple of times to distribute.

Transfer to a wide, shallow bowl, and sprinkle with the sunflower seeds, the rest of the cheese shavings, and the remaining dill and parsley.

Greek Goddess Dressing

- 1 cup (60 g) roughly chopped fresh parsley
- ½ cup (30 g) roughly chopped fresh dill
- ⅓ cup (20 g) roughly chopped fresh chives
- 4 anchovies, drained and chopped
- ¼ cup (100 g) grated Parmigiano-Reggiano
- 1 garlic clove, grated or minced
- ¼ cup (60 ml) lemon juice (about 1½ lemons)
- Zest of 1 lemon
- ½ cup (120 ml) Greek yogurt
- ½ cup (120 ml) extra-virgin olive oil
- ½ teaspoon Diamond Crystal kosher salt
- 1 teaspoon freshly ground black pepper

MAKES 2 CUPS

In the bowl of a food processor, add the parsley, dill, chives, anchovies, Parmigiano, garlic, lemon juice and zest, yogurt, and olive oil. Pulse until smooth and small flecks of green remain.

Add the salt and pepper. Pulse until combined, and adjust the seasoning to taste.

Transfer to an airtight container and refrigerate for 5 to 7 days.

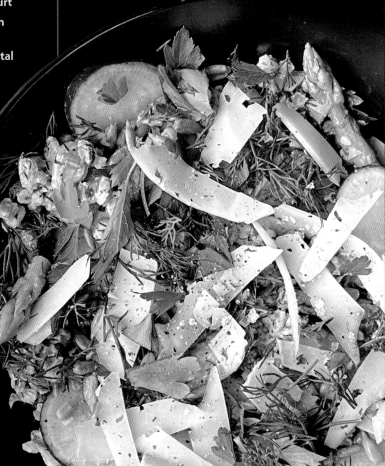

One-Pot Spring Pasta with Chèvre

SERVES 2 TO 3

The rich, creamy texture of fresh goat cheese makes for an instant sauce when tossed over hot noodles and thinned with olive oil, lemon juice, and a few splashes of salty pasta water. Raw asparagus and frozen peas are flash-cooked right in the pasta water, making for a simple one-pot preparation. Lemon zest, chives, fresh mint, and a shower of umami-rich Parmigiano bring together all the sunny flavors of high spring. You can substitute farfalle or fusilli for this, but I prefer cavatappi for its ability to hold on to the chèvre sauce. Pair with a bright red wine, chilled rosé, or lemon seltzer.

½ pound (128 g) cavatappi pasta

2 tablespoons Diamond Crystal kosher salt

1 bunch asparagus, ends removed and cut into 1-inch pieces

1 cup (160 g) frozen peas, thawed

6 ounces (170 g) chèvre

2 teaspoons olive oil

1 tablespoon freshly squeezed lemon juice

2 tablespoons chopped fresh chives

2 tablespoons chopped fresh mint

1 teaspoon lemon zest

Freshly grated Parmigiano-Reggiano, to serve

Freshly ground black pepper, to serve

Flaky salt, to serve

Fill a 4-quart (3.8-liter) pot with water and bring to a boil. Add the kosher salt.

Add the cavatappi and cook until it's just under al dente, about 5 minutes.

Add the asparagus and boil for about 30 seconds.

Add the peas, turn off the heat, and let sit for a beat. Reserve about 1 cup (240 ml) of pasta water and set aside. Drain in a colander.

Crumble the goat cheese over the hot pasta, then add the olive oil and a splash of the reserved pasta water.

Toss it all together until a sauce starts to form, adding in more pasta water a splash at a time, as needed.

Once the mixture is creamy but not loose, add the lemon juice. Taste for salt and add as needed.

Transfer to serving bowls and finish with the chives, mint, lemon zest, Parmigiano, black pepper, and flaky salt.

Ricotta Eton Mess with Rhubarb Rose Compote

SERVES 4

A traditional Eton Mess is a classic British dessert featuring macerated strawberries layered with whipped cream and meringues, similar to a parfait. When I tried my first Mess on a trip to London, I fell in love with how the crunchy meringues melted into the rich, cooling cream and sweet saucy fruit. It's a refreshing and elegant dessert that's well suited for the waxing warmth of late spring. My take features fresh ricotta whisked until fluffy and folded into honey-kissed whipped cream. The milky sweet cheese clouds are layered with vanilla meringues, fresh strawberries, and Rhubarb Rose Compote (page 129) to create an enchanting yet simple dessert. Serve alongside the Spring Tea (page 105) or May Wine (page 135).

1 cup (150 g) fresh strawberries, washed and dried , hulled, and thinly sliced

3 ounces (85 g) vanilla meringue cookies, roughly chopped

1 cup (240 ml) heavy whipping cream

1 cup (235 g) ricotta

2 teaspoons honey

½ cup (120 ml) Rhubarb Rose Compote (page 129)

Mint sprigs, to garnish

Add the cream to a large mixing bowl and beat on high with an electric mixer until it's just stiff. Scrape into a separate bowl and set aside.

Add the ricotta and honey to the mixing bowl and beat on high until fluffy. Using a spatula, gently fold the whipped cream back in until combined.

In 8-ounce (240 ml) cups or goblets, begin building the parfaits. Start with a layer of whipped ricotta, then add a teaspoon of compote. Add the strawberries and a sprinkle of chopped meringue. Layer until you get to the top and garnish with a sprig of mint. Serve immediately.

Feel free to change up the berries and compote to adjust to summer's bounty: Honey Tea-Poached Peaches (page 183) and Blackberry Protection Compote (page 183) would also shine here.

Ritual Guidance

Prepare with a visualization and
this compote is a potent fertility
spell befitting Beltane festivities.
As you massage the sugar with
the lemon zest, rose petals, and
cinnamon, imagine the energy of
the waxing sunlight infusing
into the mixture.

Rhubarb Rose Compote

MAKES ABOUT 1½ CUPS (480 G)

A spring vegetable that often gets treated like a fruit, rhubarb is ruled by Mars and associated with masculine sexuality. Combining the ruby stalks with feminine, Venusian rose petals balances the two energies and creates a tart, floral flavor that embodies the height of springtime. I love watching the fibrous vegetable transform as it cooks down with the rose petals until soft and pulpy. A little vanilla brings out the floral flavor, warming cinnamon adds depth, and lemon highlights the natural mouth-puckering tang. Enjoy on an ice cream sundae, on the Beltane Flower Plate (page 136), or in the Ricotta Eton Mess (page 126).

3 to 3½ cups (750 g to 875 g) chopped rhubarb (about 4 stalks)

⅔ cup (135 g) granulated sugar

2 teaspoons lemon zest (about 1 lemon)

½ cup (16 g) dried rose petals

⅛ teaspoon cinnamon

1 tablespoon freshly squeezed lemon juice (about ½ lemon)

½ teaspoon rose water

¼ teaspoon vanilla extract

¼ teaspoon Diamond Crystal kosher salt

Add the rhubarb and 2 tablespoons of water to a medium saucepan and bring to a simmer over medium-low heat.

In a medium bowl, combine the sugar, lemon zest, rose petals, and cinnamon. Massage them together until fragrant and the mixture has the texture of sand.

Add the sugar mixture to the rhubarb and stir clockwise, visualizing the masculine, passionate energies of Mars soaking with the sweet, lemony rose petals.

Simmer for about 15 to 20 minutes, until the rhubarb breaks down into a soft, pulpy mush. Use a wooden spoon to break up any big chunks.

Take the pan off the heat and let it cool for a few minutes.

Add the lemon juice, rose water, vanilla, and salt. Stir clockwise, asking Venus to bless the compote with loving energy.

Serve warm or let cool completely, then transfer to an airtight container and store in the fridge for about 2 weeks or freeze for 6 months.

Hot Honey

MAKES 1 CUP (340 G)

This chili-infused honey harnesses the power of the sun and the energy of balefires. Enjoyed year-round too, honey has special significance at Beltane. Bees are symbols of high spring, and their honey was offered as a libation to the fairies that emerged on Beltane. Infusing honey with chili peppers adds a little spicy depth and transforms the golden nectar into a powerful potion for protection and increasing libido. You can use any variation of either dried or fresh peppers, though the latter will significantly decrease the shelf life. I like using Thai chili or red pepper flakes, but jalapeños, serranos, or habaneros are great too. Remove any fresh peppers before storing the honey and save them for another use. (They're amazing on grilled cheese.) Serve your chili-infused honey on the Fairy Plate (page 140) or Lemon Pizza with Pesto, Prosciutto, and Smoked Gouda (page 178).

1 cup (340 g) good-quality raw honey

3 to 4 small dried or fresh chili peppers, or 1 to 2 tablespoons red pepper flakes

2 teaspoons cider vinegar (optional, but it helps keep it fresh)

Set up a double boiler: Fill a medium saucepan with water one third of the way, placing over low heat. Set a small heatproof bowl on top. Add the honey and peppers to the bowl and stir counterclockwise to incorporate, visualizing the fiery heat warding off baneful energies. Heat for about a minute, making sure the temperature does not exceed 100°F (37°F), which will kill the beneficial bacteria.

Remove the honey from the heat, and let it steep for at least an hour, or preferably overnight. Strain out the peppers (discard dried peppers, or reserve fresh peppers for another use). Stir in the vinegar if you wish, and store in an airtight container at room temperature. Hot honey will last for about a month if you're using dried chilis. If you're using fresh peppers, store in the refrigerator and it will last about 2 weeks.

Note: if you're using dried peppers and aren't in a rush, you can also do a slow infusion and skip the double boiler. Simply stir them into the honey, cover, and let infuse for at least two weeks at room temperature. Strain out the peppers before using.

Pickled Asparagus

MAKES 1 QUART (680 G)

Asparagus is one of the first vegetables to sprout out of the ground at springtime, and it arrives in abundance. The Mars-ruled phallic spears are associated with masculine energy. Unsurprisingly, they're a known aphrodisiac, often used in sex magic and fertility rituals. The asparagus harvest is abundant, and the spears are best when eaten fresh after picking, before their sugars turn to starch. Pickling is the best way to capture their energy and flavor, especially when combined with fire-ruled dill, mustard seeds, red pepper flakes, and garlic. Pair with a washed rind cheese on the Picnic Platter (page 138) or toss into the Grain Goddess Salad (page 122).

1 fresh dill sprig (about a teaspoon)

1 pound (680 g) asparagus, washed and trimmed

1 cup (240 ml) distilled white vinegar

1 cup (240 ml) water

2 tablespoons granulated sugar

1 tablespoon Diamond Crystal kosher salt

½ teaspoon red pepper flakes

¼ teaspoon mustard seeds

¼ teaspoon black peppercorns

2 garlic cloves, smashed

Place the dill inside a 1-quart mason jar, then stack the asparagus inside the jar, cut-side down.

In a medium ceramic or other nonreactive saucepan, bring the vinegar and water to a boil , then reduce to a simmer. Add the sugar, salt, red pepper flakes, mustard seeds, peppercorns, and garlic. Let simmer for 5 minutes.

Pour the hot brine into the jar, over the asparagus. Let cool completely, and cover with a lid. Turn the jar upside down a couple of times to distribute the ingredients, then store in the refrigerator overnight. They'll be ready to eat the next day.

Smoky Hibiscus Paloma

MAKES 1 COCKTAIL

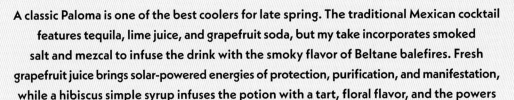

A classic Paloma is one of the best coolers for late spring. The traditional Mexican cocktail features tequila, lime juice, and grapefruit soda, but my take incorporates smoked salt and mezcal to infuse the drink with the smoky flavor of Beltane balefires. Fresh grapefruit juice brings solar-powered energies of protection, purification, and manifestation, while a hibiscus simple syrup infuses the potion with a tart, floral flavor, and the powers of healing and divination. You can also skip the smoky flavor and use standard salt and tequila instead. Serve with a creamy blue cheese or soft-ripened goat cheese.

1 tablespoon smoked salt

1 grapefruit wedge

2 ounces (60 ml) mezcal or tequila

2 ounces (60 ml) fresh grapefruit juice

¾ ounce (20 ml) Hibiscus Syrup (opposite)

½ ounce (15 ml) freshly squeezed lime juice (about half a lime)

2 ounces sparkling water

1 grapefruit wheel, to garnish

Spoon the smoked salt onto a small dish. Rub the rim of a highball glass with a grapefruit wedge and dip the rim in the salt.

Fill the glass with ice, then add the mezcal or tequila, grapefruit juice, Hibiscus Syrup, lime juice, and sparkling water. Stir for 30 seconds. Garnish with the grapefruit wheel and serve.

Ritual Guidance

Use the hibiscus for divination by reading the flowers as you would tea leaves. While cooking the syrup, ask a question out loud. While it cools, look for shapes and patterns that can provide insight into the answer.

Hibiscus Syrup

MAKES 1 CUP (240 ML)

1 cup (200 g) granulated sugar

1 teaspoon lime zest (about 1 lime)

½ cup (16 g) dried hibiscus flowers

¼ teaspoon smoked salt

Add the sugar and lime zest to a small bowl. Massage with your fingers until the mixture is fragrant and sandy.

Fill a saucepan with a cup of water and add the hibiscus. Bring to a simmer over medium-low heat and add the lime-infused sugar and salt. Cook for 10 minutes and remove from the heat. Let cool completely, then strain and store in an airtight container in the fridge. It will last about 2 weeks.

Note

Woodruff is difficult to substitute and tricky to find. I suggest ordering it online from a specialty herbalist.

May Wine

MAKES ABOUT 3 CUPS (750 ML)

This classic Beltane beverage hails from Germany, where it's known as Maiwein. It's a simple potion made of white wine steeped with woodruff, a woodland herb that takes on aromas of vanilla and sweet hay when dried. Traditionally, May wine uses German Riesling, especially from the Rhone Valley. I prefer Riesling Trocken, but you can use any dry white wine such as Pinot Gris or Gewürztraminer. Mixed with lemon zest–perfumed honey and garnished with strawberries, my take on May Wine drinks like a lusty nectar with a similar flavor profile to that of a sippable vermouth. Pair with the blossom-infused cheeses on the Beltane Flower Plate (page 136) or with a mild, creamy blue, such as Bleu d'Auvergne.

3 cups (750 ml) white wine, preferably Riesling Trocken

⅓ cup (16 g) dried woodruff

1 tablespoon honey

1 teaspoon lemon zest

2 tablespoons warm water

4–6 sliced fresh strawberries, to garnish

Pour the wine into a jar or carafe, and add the dried woodruff. Stir three times, visualizing the fertile energy of high spring infusing into the wine.

To a small measuring cup, add the honey and lemon zest. Stir in the water until the honey melts and a thin syrup forms.

Pour the honey syrup into the wine and stir three times, imagining the waxing sunlight infusing into the wine.

Place in the fridge for a few hours or overnight.

Strain the wine over a fine-mesh sieve.

Serve in stemmed glasses, chilled or over ice, garnished with the sliced strawberries.

1 Tête de Moine

is a washed-rind cheese from the Alps. Her name is French for "head of the monk," referencing the wheel's resemblance to the bald spot on a monk's head when the top rind is shaved off to form razor-thin cheese flowers. These ruffled blossoms don't just look gorgeous, they provide a larger surface area, which allows the bold, brothy flavors to gently unfold across your palate. Pair with almonds to tease out her nutty notes.

2 Trillium

is a triple cream Brie-style cheese from Tulip Tree, an Indiana-based creamery that names all of its cheeses after flowers. The white, downy rind encases a rich, creamy interior that becomes soft and spreadable as it ages. She's as indulgent as a slice of cheesecake, especially when paired with a dollop of rhubarb. If you can't find her, look for any small-format triple cream Brie like Mt Tam or Brillat-Saverin.

3 Fresh chèvre rolled in flowers

complements the grassy flavors of goat cheese with floral notes, while adding a touch of whimsy to the plate. Pair with honey and crackers.

HONEY

is the nectar of pollinating bees, the true essence of flowers derived from millions of blossoms. To represent the heat from the balefires, use Hot Honey (page 130).

RASPBERRIES

are a tart and juicy, pairing with the tangy chèvre and salty almonds.

FLOWER COATING

Fill a small dish with an assortment of edible dried petals. You'll want about a teaspoon per ounce of chèvre. Mix the petals together, then pat them into a flat, even layer. Roll your goat cheese into a log, and place it on the plate of flowers. Gently press the petals into the cheese until full coated, leaving the ends bare.

SESAME CREAM CRACKERS

(page 99) offer a crisp, buttery bed for the soft chèvre and luscious triple cream.

1

RHUBARB ROSE
COMPOTE

(page 129) brings fertile
energy and a bright tang,
which cuts through the
richness of the cheeses.

THE BELTANE FLOWER PLATE

This floral-themed cheese plate
celebrates the abundance of flowers
and fertile energy that Beltane brings.
The festival of high spring already
has a special association with florals,
with blossoms exploding across the
landscape and adorning tables,
flower crowns, and even fashion.
The ancient Romans held a festival
called Floralia around the same
time as Beltane. It honored Flora,
the goddess of flowers, with
singing, dancing, and the drinking
of a potent flower-based wine. This
platter honors the beauty of spring
florals with petal-coated cheese,
blossoms made of cheese, rose-
scented compote, and the nectar of
pollen-drunk bees, along with other
flower-friendly components. Serve
with a carafe of May Wine (page
135) and raise a toast to high spring.

2

ALMONDS

are popular in fertility
spells, and their
fragrant oil is often
used in beauty rituals.
The almond tree is also

has the right amount
of acidity and bite to
contrast with the fatty
cheese while teasing
out the brothy flavors.

THE PICNIC PLATTER

As the sun's waxing light warms the earth, nature beckons us to join her and lounge on the soft new grass. This board is designed to accompany you outdoors, with sturdy cheeses that can withstand a couple of hours in the sun. Hard cheeses, especially ones made with sheep's milk, are known to sweat: their rich butterfat pools on their surface and forever alters the texture. The cheeses featured here soften instead, relaxing under the sunlight onto torn pieces of crusty baguette. There are no messy jams or sticky honeys, just a little mustard and salami to complement the savory notes in the cheeses. Fresh grapes, sugar snap peas, and juicy Pickled Asparagus (page 131) offer a crisp, refreshing break between the bites of richness. Pair with sparkling wine, a berry-forward seltzer, or a pale ale.

1

SEEDED BAGUETTE

brings a crusty texture
and yeasty notes that
complement the washed
rind cheese while
contrasting with her
custardy texture.

SUGAR SNAP PEAS

represent the
abundant and fertile
energy of high spring
due to their verdant
green color.

GRAPES

plump and sensual, offer a sweet, refreshing respite from the salty plate.

CHIVE BLOSSOMS

add a pop of color and savory aroma.

2

PICKLED ASPARAGUS

(page 131) provides a briny crunch that cuts through the rich cheeses.

SOPPRESSATA

complements the meaty flavors in the washed rind and the savory notes in the semi-firm cheese.

1 A pudgy washed rind cheese

offers savory, brothy flavors and a soft, plush texture. Look for the classic Munster Gerome (pictured) or Oma from von Trapp Farmstead. Layer a thick slice onto the baguette with a dollop of mustard.

2 A semi-firm, natural rind cow's milk cheese

brings a sunny golden hue and notes of cultured butter, toasted nuts, and a forest-y funk near the rind. Look for the French Tomme de Savoie or Appalachian from Meadow Creek Dairy in Virginia (pictured) and pair it with salami and pickled asparagus.

1   Cashel

is the first blue cheese made in Ireland, the land of the fae. She's voluptuous and mild mannered, with gentle blue notes punctuating her rich, buttery flavor. Her milky sweetness complements the strawberries, while her salinity longs for a drizzle of honey and a sweet, buttery Mini Oat Pancake.

2   Soft-ripened chèvre

offers a cake-like texture and tart, milky flavors that pair beautifully with the Turkish delight and pistachios. I recommend a chèvre with a delicate gossamer rind such as French Chabichou or Cremont from Vermont Creamery (pictured). I also love this plate with the pudgy, flower-coated Julianna from Capriole Goat Cheese in Indiana.

TURKISH DELIGHT

is chewy, sweet, and perfumed with rose water, which is known to attract fairies.

THYME

offers protection and infuses the plate with a woodsy aroma reminiscent of an enchanted forest.

HONEY

is one of the fae's favorite libations, and its sweet nectar contrasts with the salty cheeses.

Pistachios pair with
the berries and are
delicious crushed
and crumbled over
the cheeses.

2

THE
FAIRY
PLATE

Many ancient Celts marked the change of
seasons during the cross-quarter festivals,
rather than the equinoxes and solstices.
Some also only observed two seasons:
winter, which began at Samhain, and
summer, marked by the arrival of Beltane.
The Celts believed that during these festivals, the veil between worlds was thin.
While Samhain opened the door to the
spirit world, Beltane brought a portal into
the land of the fae, also known as fairies.

We generally think of fairies as lovely
little nymph-like creatures with glittery
wings and the magical ability to grant
wishes, but historically, they are known
for causing mischief and meddling in
people's affairs. To appease the fae and
ask for blessings during the harvest,
people would leave offerings during
Beltane. As the fairies loved all things
sweet, these little gifts included berries,
honey, cakes, and candies, all of which are
represented on this fairy-inspired plate.
Pair with the Smoky Hibiscus Paloma
(page 132) to call in the energy of balefires
and protect yourself from their mischief.

STRAWBERRIES

are a sweet contrast
that plays off the salty
blue and honey.

MINI OAT PANCAKES

(page 117) are traditional
Beltane fare and their
miniature size makes for
a fitting offering to the fae.

LITHA

Named after the Old English word for June, Litha celebrates the summer solstice. The sun has climbed to her highest point in the sky and her energy peaks as her light shines over the longest day of the year. Midsummer is a time for feasting, merriment, and rest before the earth goddess gives birth to her bounty and the difficult work of the harvest commences. Nurture what's sprouting, gather your loved ones for a feast, and enjoy the serene summer days while they last, for darkness lurks around the corner. If the winter solstice marks the birth of the sun, the summer solstice marks her death, for tomorrow she begins her descent.

Herbal Magic

The Druids believed that magical herbs were most potent at midsummer, blessed by the sun at her peak power. Before the sunlight began to wane, they'd harvest herbs such as Saint-John's-wort, heather, and, most importantly, mistletoe. While it is commonly used as Yule decor in the modern age, the Druids considered mistletoe one of the most sacred herbs for healing and divination. Unfortunately, it's poisonous, so we're honoring this ritual with edible kitchen herbs that taste of early summer.

Savory Comté Dutch Baby

SERVES 2 TO 3

This savory take on the classic baked pancake incorporates the bounty of herbs in season during the summer solstice. Chives, parsley, and thyme bring a bright, verdant flavor to the pancake and tease out the herbaceous notes in the Comté. Serve with coffee or the Garlic Bloody Mary (page 106).

3 large eggs, at room temperature

½ cup (60 g) all-purpose flour

½ cup (120 ml) milk, at room temperature

2 teaspoons granulated sugar

1 teaspoon Diamond Crystal kosher salt, plus more for seasoning

½ teaspoon freshly ground black pepper, plus more for seasoning

⅛ teaspoon nutmeg

2 teaspoons chopped fresh thyme

2 tablespoons chopped fresh chives

2 tablespoons unsalted butter

½ cup (55 g) shredded Comté, medium grate

⅓ cup (10 g) fresh parsley leaves, chopped

1 teaspoon olive oil

½ teaspoon freshly squeezed lemon juice

Place a 10-inch (25-cm) skillet in the oven. Set to 425°F (220°C) and preheat for 20 minutes.

To a blender, add the eggs, flour, milk, sugar, salt, pepper, nutmeg, thyme, and chives. Pulse until just combined.

Let the batter rest for 10 minutes, then give it an extra pulse.

Remove the skillet from the oven and add the butter. As it melts, swirl it around the pan, making sure to coat all sides.

Pour the batter in a swirl around the edges of the pan. Return to the oven and bake for 15 minutes.

Reduce the heat to 300°F (148°C). Remove the pancake from the oven and sprinkle with the grated cheese. Return to the oven and bake for 5 more minutes, or until it's puffed and browned.

Meanwhile, add the parsley to a small bowl along with the olive oil and lemon juice, and season to taste with the salt and pepper. Gently toss and set aside.

Remove from the oven and let cool for a minute or two. Garnish with the parsley salad, slice like a pizza, and serve immediately.

Marinated Mozzarella Pearls

MAKES ONE 8-OUNCE (240 ML) JAR

Fresh mozzarella is a summer staple. Milky and mild, she makes for a lovely canvas for more flavorful ingredients, and she's available in a variety of sizes. I love the perlini, which are so tiny that they're named after pearls. Their small surface area makes them perfect for marinating, readily soaking up the flavorful oil like little sponges. There's something quite oceanic about mozzarella, from the salty brine in which she's stored to her luminescent glow.

When you finish off the cheese, be sure to save the leftover oil. It makes a delicious dip for bread or a base for a vinaigrette. Pair with a bed of greens dressed with the marinating oil, toasted ciabatta, and a chilled glass of Rosato (Italian rosé). If you want to take it up a notch, drizzle the pearls with a little balsamic vinegar before serving.

8 ounces (225 g) mozzarella pearls, drained

¾ cup (180 ml) extra-virgin olive oil

¼ cup (60 ml) grapeseed oil

3 garlic cloves, minced

2 anchovies, minced

1 tablespoon chopped fresh basil

1 teaspoon red pepper flakes

½ tablespoon dried oregano

½ teaspoon freshly ground black pepper

1 bay leaf

Drain the mozzarella pearls, and transfer to an 8-ounce (240-ml) jar.

Pour the olive and grapeseed oils into a liquid measuring cup and whisk together. Add the garlic, anchovies, basil, red pepper flakes, oregano, black pepper, and bay leaf.

Pour the mixture over the mozzarella, cover, and refrigerate for at least 2 hours, preferably 12. It will keep in the fridge for up to a week. Let sit at room temperature for at least 15 minutes before serving.

Note: If you're in a rush, add the oils to a saucepan and heat over medium-low. Add the flavorings and gently simmer for 5 minutes. Let cool completely, then pour over the mozzarella and marinate for 20 minutes.

Customize the Flavors

Since Litha launches Cancer season, which is ruled by the moon, I'm running with the water sign energy with salty anchovies. If you're not into them, feel free to omit the salty little fishes. You can play with all of the flavorings, but I caution against subbing out the grapeseed oil, which prevents the olive oil from solidifying while the pearls steep in the fridge.

Summer Squash

⊶○───────○⊷

Summer squash is one of the most abundant vegetables out there. They grow easily in nearly any soil and flourish even when neglected. They also flower more than a lot of other crops and have a cyclical growing cycle, meaning the more you harvest, the more they'll produce. Unsurprisingly, this resilient and prolific vegetable is a popular ingredient in money magic and prosperity rituals. Associated with earth energy, zucchini is also a spiritual match with bright, grassy cilantro, which highlights its flavor.

Grilled Zucchini Salad with Lime, Cilantro, and Cotija

SERVES 4

Zucchini is native to Mexico, dating back to at least 5500 BC, and this salad honors that heritage with Cotija. Named after the town of the same name in the Michoacán region, Cotija has a salty, milky flavor and crumbly texture that makes it a popular topping for grilled dishes like elote. Here, it tops grilled zucchini planks, finished with lime juice and a little Tajín for heat. It's a simple salad, but with the amount of zucchini that's to come throughout the harvest season, you need something easy. Pair with a light beer or the Solstice Sun Tea (page 159).

2 pounds (910 g) zucchini, washed and dried

2 teaspoons Diamond Crystal kosher salt, divided

2 tablespoons olive oil

¼ cup (16 g) chopped fresh cilantro

1½ tablespoons toasted pepitas

½ lime

2 ounces (55 g) Cotija Añejo

Tajín, to finish

Cut the zucchini lengthwise into ¼-inch (6-cm) slices. Lay out on a baking sheet, sprinkle with 1 teaspoon of the salt, and let sit for 10 minutes. Use a paper towel to wipe off the salt and moisture.

Flip the zucchini and repeat on the other side.

Add the zucchini to a large bowl, then add the olive oil. Toss to coat.

Heat the grill to medium-high heat, about 400°F (200°C). Spread out the zucchini, and grill until tender and charred, about 5 minutes on each side. Let cool for about 5 minutes.

Spread out over a serving platter. Sprinkle with the cilantro and pepitas and squeeze the lime over it all. Grate the Cotija over, then finish with a dusting of Tajín. Serve immediately.

Yogurt Sauce

1 cup (240 ml) Greek yogurt

4 ounces (115 g) feta, roughly chopped

Zest of 1 lemon

1 garlic clove, grated

Freshly ground black pepper

Kosher salt

MAKES 1 CUP

In the bowl of a food processor, add the yogurt, feta, lemon zest, grated garlic, and a pinch of freshly ground black pepper. Pulse until smooth, then taste for seasoning, and add salt and pepper as needed.

Feta-Brined Grilled Chicken Thighs

SERVES 4

Ancient peoples throughout northern Europe celebrated the summer solstice with bonfires to honor the sun and strengthen its power, ensuring an abundant harvest season. Midsummer is also a time of extroversion, when we gather with families and friends to enjoy the lazy days of summer. You can honor both these rituals by lighting up the grill, inviting your loved ones, and preparing a feast featuring these feta-brined chicken thighs. It's a great way to use up the brine left over from a tub of feta. Similar to a yogurt- or buttermilk-based marinade, feta brine slowly tenderizes the meat and keeps it juicy. The crispy thighs are also served with a bed of garlicky Greek yogurt and finished with grilled lemon. Serve with a glass of Solstice Sun Tea (page 159).

2 pounds (910 g) chicken thighs

8 ounces (240 ml) feta brine

6 garlic cloves, roughly chopped

¼ cup (16 g) chopped fresh parsley, plus more for garnish

3 tablespoons Greek yogurt

1 tablespoon oregano

1 teaspoon cumin

½ teaspoon coriander

¼ teaspoon cayenne pepper

1 teaspoon Diamond Crystal kosher salt

1 teaspoon freshly ground black pepper

1 whole lemon, sliced in half

1 cup Yogurt Sauce (opposite)

Pat the chicken thighs dry and set aside.

In a large bowl, mix the feta brine with the chopped garlic, parsley, Greek yogurt, oregano, cumin, coriander, cayenne, salt, and pepper. Add the chicken and mix until fully coated. Cover and refrigerate for at least 2 hours, or preferably overnight.

Let the chicken sit at room temperature for at least 10 minutes. Heat your grill to medium-high, or about 400°F (200°C).

Shake off the excess marinade, add the chicken to the grill, and cook until charred, about 6 to 8 minutes.

Place the lemon halves on the grill, then flip the chicken. Grill until the chicken is cooked through and the lemon is charred, about another 6 minutes. Let rest for 5 minutes. Meanwhile, make the yogurt sauce.

Smear the yogurt sauce over a serving platter. Layer the chicken on top and garnish with the extra chopped parsley. Add the charred lemon halves to the platter and serve.

Blue Cheese Ice Cream with Caramel Ribbons

MAKES 1 QUART (975 G)

The trick to making cheesy ice cream is a custard base, which includes egg yolks. The added richness marries the savory cheese flavor with the sweet ice cream. Making custard might seem intimidating, but it's easier than you think. You just need to remember to whisk constantly as you pour the heated milk into the yolks, which prevents the eggs from cooking. Also, don't let the custard come to a full boil or the mixture will be too thick—we're looking for a gentle simmer here. I recommend using a blue cheese with a soft, creamy texture, like Bleu d'Auvergne or Maytag. Serve on its own or atop a warm baked brownie or cherry pie.

4 ounces (115 g) blue cheese

1 cup (240 ml) whole milk

⅔ cup (135 g) granulated sugar

4 egg large yolks

1 cup (240 ml) heavy whipping cream

¼ cup (60 ml) caramel sauce, such cajeta

Crumble the cheese into a medium bowl. You want the crumbles to be small enough so they melt into the hot custard. Place a sieve on top and set aside.

Set a saucepan over low heat and add the milk and sugar. Whisk until the sugar dissolves and the milk is steamy.

Add the egg yolks to a medium mixing bowl and whisk until smooth.

Slowly ladle about ½ cup of the warm milk mixture into the yolks, whisking constantly to prevent the yolks from cooking.

Scrape the mixture back into the saucepan and heat over medium-low heat. Use a spatula to stir constantly, being careful to scrape across the bottom of the saucepan to make sure the custard is cooking evenly.

Let cook until the mixture thickens, about 5 minutes.

You'll know it's done when you run your finger down the back of the spatula and the line of custard remains rather than running back together.

Strain the mixture through the sieve, right over the cheese. Stir the mixture until the cheese mostly melts. It doesn't need to be completely smooth—a couple of tiny crumbles are delightful—but you want the flavors to fully incorporate.

Whisk in the cream, then chill thoroughly in the fridge. Finish the recipe according to your ice cream maker's instructions, churning until the ice cream is the texture of soft serve.

Meanwhile, microwave the caramel in 5-second intervals until it's soft enough to drizzle but not so hot that it will melt the ice cream.

Spoon some of the ice cream into a freezer-friendly container, making an even layer about an inch thick. Drizzle a generous portion of the caramel over the ice cream, then top with another layer of ice cream. Repeat until the container is full, ending with a top layer of ice cream.

Note:

The technique for this recipe is adapted from a Roquefort Honey Ice Cream made by David Lebovitz.

Feta-Stuffed Peppers

MAKES 20 TO 30 PEPPERS

These pickled piquanté peppers are stuffed with garlic and thyme-infused whipped feta for a refreshing and tangy finger food that's best enjoyed poolside with a glass of chilled wine. I love how easy it all is: you're basically just filling peppers with garlicky feta dip, which is all the effort I want to exert on a lazy summer day. Serve with a gin martini, with a glass of sauvignon blanc, or on the Antipasto Plate (page 163).

6 ounces (175 g) feta

2 garlic cloves, minced

2 teaspoons chopped fresh thyme

2 tablespoons olive oil, plus more for covering

½ teaspoon Diamond Crystal kosher salt, plus more to taste

½ teaspoon freshly ground black pepper, plus more to taste

1 jar pickled piquanté peppers (about 20 to 30 peppers)

Crumble the feta into the bowl of a food processor. Add the garlic, thyme, and olive oil. Process until smooth and creamy.

Add the salt and pepper. Taste, and season with more to your liking.

Scrape into a frosting bag or plastic bag. Cut the corner off so that the opening is about ¼ inch.

Pipe the filling into the peppers. Place into a wide-mouthed jar and cover with olive oil. Chill for about an hour and serve.

Kath's Famous Pesto

MAKES ABOUT 1½ CUPS (90 G)

Pesto is a true summer staple and the perfect way to use up an abundance of basil. This recipe comes from my mom. It's a little different from the classic, but it's the best pesto I've ever eaten. In addition to basil, Kath adds a hefty dose of parsley, which brings an extra zip and helps maintain the green color. Toss with pasta, serve on the Antipasto Plate (page 164), or make Lemon Pizza with Pesto, Prosciutto, and Smoked Gouda (page 178).

½ cup (65 g) pine nuts

2 to 3 cloves garlic

2 cups (80 g) tightly packed fresh basil leaves

1 cup (50 g) tightly packed parsley leaves

1 cup (100 g) Parmigiano, grated

1 ½ teaspoons kosher salt

1 teaspoon black pepper, freshly ground

1 cup (240 ml) extra-virgin olive oil

Heat a medium skillet over medium-low heat. Add the pine nuts and toast, stirring occasionally, until browned, about 5 minutes.

In the bowl of a food processor, combine the garlic and nuts. Pulse until smooth. Add the basil, parsley, Parmigiano, salt, and pepper. Pulse to combine.

Pour the oil in slowly, pulsing as you go.

Taste and add more salt if needed. Store in an airtight container in the fridge for about 1 week or freeze for up to 6 months.

This recipe was first published in my debut book, Cheese Sex Death: A Bible for the Cheese Obsessed.

Note

Blackberries are naturally rich
in phytochemicals, which are
produced by plants to protect
them from viruses and pathogens.
Studies suggest that they are
anti-inflammatory and antiviral
and contain compounds that
can protect against heart
disease and even cancer.

Blackberry Protection Compote

MAKES ABOUT 1 CUP (320 G)

In magic, blackberries are used to protect against evil spirits, especially because of the plant's thorny branches. Their woodsy flavor is a natural pairing with rosemary, a potently medicinal herb that's commonly used in protection and healing spells. Black salt wards off any lingering dark energies, while honey brings solar power as well as its own antibacterial and antifungal properties. Pair with pudgy washed rind cheeses and aged Alpine styles or serve on the Protection Plate (page 166).

¼ cup (50 g) granulated sugar

2 teaspoons lemon zest

1 teaspoon chopped fresh rosemary

2 cups (300 g) fresh blackberries

2 teaspoons cornstarch

2 teaspoons freshly squeezed lemon juice

1 tablespoon honey

¼ teaspoon black salt

Add the sugar, lemon zest, and rosemary to a small bowl. Massage the mixture with your fingertips, imagining the protective powers of the lemon and rosemary infusing into the sugar.

When the sugar mixture resembles the texture of wet sand, transfer to a small saucepan with the blackberries and heat over low. Cook until the sugar melts and the berries are soft and soupy, 10 minutes. Use your spoon to mash the berries as they cook, to release their juices.

In a separate small bowl, mix the cornstarch with the lemon juice until a slurry forms. Add to the blackberries and stir to incorporate. Cook until the compote has thickened, another 5 minutes.

Remove from the heat and let cool for 5 minutes. Add the honey and black salt and stir to combine.

Store in an airtight container in the fridge for 7 to 10 days or freeze for up to 6 months.

Cilantro Jalapeño Syrup

2 jalapeños, seeded and sliced

12 sprigs fresh cilantro, rinsed

1 cup (200 g) granulated sugar

¼ teaspoon Diamond Crystal kosher salt

MAKES 1 RECIPE

Fill a saucepan with 1 cup of water and bring to a simmer. Add the jalapeños, cilantro, sugar, and salt. Bring to a simmer and let cook for 10 minutes. Remove from the heat, strain, and let cool completely. The syrup will keep in the fridge for up to 2 weeks.

Solstice Sun Tea

MAKES 1 QUART (946 ML)

This iced tea is aglow with solar power: infused with black tea, calendula, and sunlight, then sweetened with a spicy Cilantro Jalapeño Syrup and brightened with lime juice. It is crafted not only to taste like summer, but to prepare you to get the most out of the season. Calendula is associated with sun energy and is used to strengthen spells and instill confidence. Lime is traditionally used in cleansing and healing, especially since it's naturally rich in vitamin C. Cilantro is popular in fertility rituals, and jalapeño is used for protection and to speed up any spell—from love to luck and success. Pair with an aged Pecorino or serve alongside The Litha Sun Plate (page 162).

2 tablespoons dried calendula

5 black tea bags

Juice of 1 lime

Cilantro Jalapeño Syrup

Lime wheels, to garnish

Add the calendula to an empty tea bag or strainer and place it inside a mason jar or pitcher. Add the black tea bags and fill with a quart of water. Place the jar or pitcher in the sunlight and let it sit for at least 3 hours.

When the tea is done steeping, remove the tea bags. Add the lime juice, then add the syrup to taste. Pour the brew into ice-filled glasses, and garnish with the lime wheels.

Note: Making sun tea is an age-old summer tradition that's become unpopular due to the possibility of bacterial growth. To stay on the safe side, let the tea and calendula sit in the sun for several hours before brewing. Then continue with the recipe, but leave the pitcher in the refrigerator to cold-brew for about 12 hours.

Orange Blossom Lemonade

SERVES 4

Much like its fruit, the blossoms of the orange tree are traditionally associated with love, luck, prosperity, and divination. They also contain much of the same properties of oranges and can instill joy and happiness. Mixed with lemon juice, orange blossom water makes for a delicious and refreshing beverage that tastes like liquid sunshine. Drink it to lift your spirits, call back your energy, or boost confidence. The bright, sunny flavor and purifying powers are an ideal pairing with the Protection Plate (page 166).

1 cup (200 g) granulated sugar

3 tablespoons lemon zest (about 3 lemons)

1 teaspoon orange blossom water

1 cup (240 ml) freshly squeezed lemon juice (5 to 7 lemons)

1 cup ice

4 lemon wheels, for serving

Combine the sugar and lemon zest in a medium bowl. Rub together with your fingers, envisioning the purifying essence of the lemon uniting with the sweetness of the sugar. When the mixture resembles the texture of fine sand, transfer it to a saucepan.

Add 1 cup (120 ml) of water to a small saucepan, bring to a simmer, and cook for 5 minutes, stirring occasionally. Let the syrup cool completely, then strain into a jar. Cover and cool in the refrigerator, or store it for up to 10 days.

When ready to serve, add the syrup, orange blossom water, lemon juice, 1 cup (240 ml) of water and ice to a blender and pulse to combine. Fill four glasses with ice, then pour the lemonade over. Garnish each with a lemon wheel and serve.

The Summer Solstice

Midsummer has been celebrated by ancient people around the world.

UNITED KINGDOM

In the UK, the famous Stonehenge was built to align with the movement of the sun, and functioned as a site for ritual and ceremony. While it fell into disuse for thousands of years, nowadays people come from all over the world to watch as the sun rises to the northeast of the iconic monument.

EUROPE

Many European countries celebrate midsummer a few days after the solstice, believing it to be a liminal time when fairies, trolls, and other magical creatures had free roam of the human realm, as depicted in Shakespeare's *A Midsummer Night's Dream*. In some countries, it's tradition to light a wheel on fire and let it roll down a hill into a body of water.

EGYPT

The ancient Egyptians celebrated Ra, the sun god and creator of life. From the view of the sphinx, the sun would set perfectly between the pyramids on the day of the solstice.

CHINA

In ancient China, the summer solstice coincided with the wheat harvest and was a time for giving gratitude for the earth's bounty by eating cold noodles.

1 Bay Blue

from Point Reyes Farmstead Cheese Company in California, is similar to Stilton, only younger and sweeter. She has the texture of fudge and an oatmeal cookie–like sweetness with a gentle oceanic brininess and spicy pockets of blue molds marbled throughout. She's a summertime favorite of mine and a perfect match for sunflower seed bread and juicy pineapple.

2 Cotija Añejo

comes from the mountains of Jalisco and Michoacán in Mexico. While most of us are more familiar with fresh Cotija, the Añejo version, which is Spanish for "old," is made with raw milk during the rainy season and aged for at least two months. She crumbles at the touch and has salty notes of fresh milk. The best wheels are hay colored and taste of toasted nuts and wet soil. Pair with Sungold tomatoes and a little lime.

3 Panela cheese

has a springy texture and mild flavor, similar to other grilling cheeses such as Juustoleipä or Halloumi. Panela was originally made using the same molds that shaped the conical raw sugar of the same name, and is perfect for grilling and frying because she holds her shape and doesn't melt. Crisp her up in a buttered frying pan or throw her on the grill and pair her with a slice of mango and a drizzle of hot honey.

PINEAPPLE symbolizes hospitality and offers protective energies, thanks to its armor of scales.

SUNGOLD TOMATOES bring a sunny hue, and the savory flavor plays off the salty Cotija.

LIME SLICES ward off negative energies and call in abundance.

SUNFLOWER SEED BREAD is a dark, rustic German bread that pairs perfectly with the blue cheese and a little hot honey.

2

MANGOES

act as a juicy palate
cleanser and signify
sensuality, fertility,
and divination.

THE LITHA SUN PLATE

Summer has officially arrived, and the earth is
vibrating with vitality and endless possibility.
Litha is the fieriest of all the festivals because
it honors the solar power that illuminates the
darkness, heats the earth, feeds the plants,
cleanses, and charges. It's an opportunity to
celebrate the sun at her peak and to seize the
day, before the waxing darkness swallows
the earth in shadows. The Litha Sun Plate is
essentially an altar to the sun, built to honor
her power and wish her a safe, short journey
into the underworld. Enjoy outdoors in the
sunshine with a freshly brewed pitcher
of Solstice Sun Tea (page 159).

HOT HONEY

(page 130) brings a
little heat and rich,
solar-powered
sweetness.

3

CILANTRO

brings earth energy and a
bright, verdant flavor that
complements both the
Cotija and Panela.

KATH'S FAMOUS PESTO

(page 155) is perfect for spreading onto the ciabatta and pairing with the Taleggio.

CIABATTA

acts as a neutral bed for the pesto and flavorful oil left behind by the marinated mozzarella.

THE ANTI–PASTO PLATE

Antipasto, meaning "before the meal," is an Italian ritual of serving finger foods as an appetizer. Like most Italian cuisine, the specifics of an antipasto vary greatly from region to region. Sometimes it includes tiny, bite-sized portions, while in other areas the ritual is much more extensive and can take upwards of an hour to serve and consume. Usually, antipasti include cold bites, like cheeses, charcuterie, and pickled or marinated vegetables. I love how this style of platter is both indulgent and perfect for grazing on a hot, lazy summer day. Since Litha celebrates the final opportunity to rest and luxuriate before harvest season commences, the Antipasto Plate is a perfect way to enjoy the solstice. Serve with lots of chilled Lambrusco, Rosato, or a limonata soda.

COPPA

also known as capicola or gabagool, is a dry-cured, whole-muscle meat that's often coated with seasonings like fennel and red pepper.

DRIED FIGS

add a sensual, fertile energy and a little sweetness to offset the savory flavors on the platter.

CALABRESE PICCANTE

is a spicy pork salami that's delicious with pesto and Taleggio.

FETA-STUFFED PEPPERS

(page 154) add a pop of color and savory aroma.

CHERRY TOMATOES

bring a juicy burst of freshness, which breaks up the other indulgent, oily accompaniments.

OLIVES

are associated with solar energy and abundance, and bring a bright, briny flavor that contrasts with the rich cheeses.

MARCONA ALMONDS

bring a salty crunch and a little nutty note that pairs well with the Parmigiano.

1 Marinated Mozzarella Pearls

(page 146) are mild, refreshing, and dripping with a spicy, anchovy-infused olive oil. They're delicious on a slice of ciabatta with lemony sardines or speared on a toothpick with cherry tomatoes.

2 Taleggio

is one of the most iconic washed rind cheeses, beloved for her pudgy, custard-like texture and mild funk. She's soft, squishy, and square-shaped with a rusty orange rind that develops stripes of grayish mold. She smells yeasty, with notes of baking bread followed by earthy mushrooms and a subtle beefy aroma.

3 Parmigiano-Reggiano

is known as the king of cheese and dates back to Roman times. Records suggest the recipe hasn't changed much in 900 years. Since its production is closely regulated by the Italian government, every wedge of authentic Parm is great; however, the best wheels are euphoric, bursting with notes of pineapple, roasted walnuts, and a salty, umami-laden finish. Look for Vacche Rossa, made with milk from an heirloom breed of cow, or a wedge aged by the legendary affineurs Giorgio Cravero.

1 | Valençay

is a pyramid-shaped chèvre from the Loire Valley in central France. She's a beautiful charcoal gray, resulting from a coating of vegetable ash that helps her wrinkled rind develop as she ages. Her snow-white interior is velvety and cloud-like, melting in your mouth with a lemon-tart, mineral-rich flavor. If you can't find Valençay, look for Humboldt Fog from Cypress Grove in California, Wabash Cannonball from Capriole Goat Cheese in Indiana, or any other ash-ripened goat cheese.

BLACKBERRY PROTECTION COMPOTE

(page 157) features two highly protective ingredients with woodsy notes that complement the tangy cheese.

WALNUTS

are resilient, especially due to their thick, protective shells, and they also taste incredible with both the blackberry compote and fresh berries.

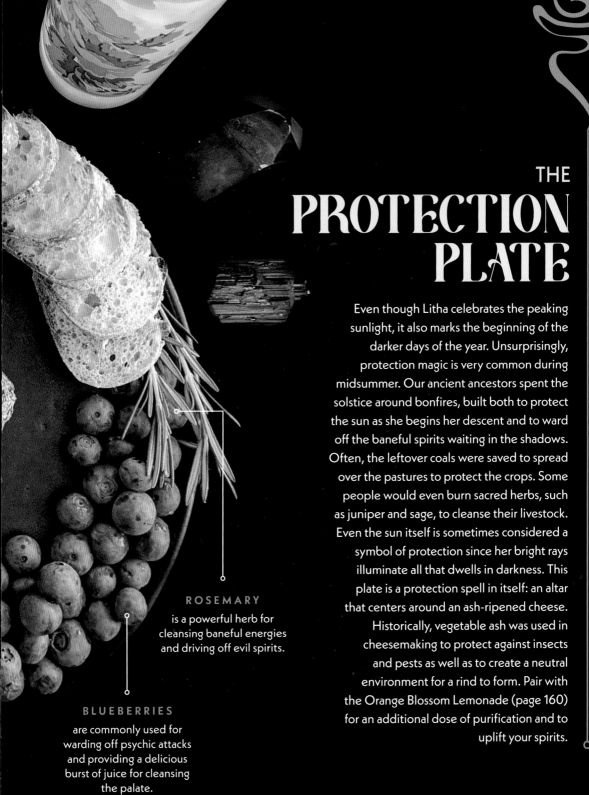

THE
PROTECTION
PLATE

Even though Litha celebrates the peaking sunlight, it also marks the beginning of the darker days of the year. Unsurprisingly, protection magic is very common during midsummer. Our ancient ancestors spent the solstice around bonfires, built both to protect the sun as she begins her descent and to ward off the baneful spirits waiting in the shadows. Often, the leftover coals were saved to spread over the pastures to protect the crops. Some people would even burn sacred herbs, such as juniper and sage, to cleanse their livestock. Even the sun itself is sometimes considered a symbol of protection since her bright rays illuminate all that dwells in darkness. This plate is a protection spell in itself: an altar that centers around an ash-ripened cheese. Historically, vegetable ash was used in cheesemaking to protect against insects and pests as well as to create a neutral environment for a rind to form. Pair with the Orange Blossom Lemonade (page 160) for an additional dose of purification and to uplift your spirits.

ROSEMARY

is a powerful herb for cleansing baneful energies and driving off evil spirits.

BLUEBERRIES

are commonly used for warding off psychic attacks and providing a delicious burst of juice for cleansing the palate.

LUGHNASADH

The first of the harvest holidays, Lughnasadh celebrates the arrival of grain. Though the name is derived from the Old Irish word for August, Lunasa, the festival didn't always fall on a specific day. The celebration started when the difficult work of the harvest began. The seeds planted in spring have grown and ripened into wheat, barley, oats, and corn, ready to be milled and baked into breads or even brewed into beer. It's a season marked by abundance, a time to express gratitude for the fruits of the earth while savoring the last days of summer. The portal to autumn is open, the daylight shrinks back into darkness, and we must gather what we need to sustain us through the barren months to come.

Kimchi BEC

MAKES 2 SANDWICHES

People usually assume that cheese professionals turn up their noses at processed American slices, but that's a myth. The truth is nothing melts like good old American cheese, and I think she shines best on a classic BEC (aka bacon, egg, and cheese). My go-to breakfast sandwich also involves a few slices of ripe avocado, some chopped kimchi, and a savory sauce made with mayo and a little kimchi brine. It's a mouthwatering combination best enjoyed alongside a hot cup of black coffee or green tea.

2 English muffins, split

2 tablespoons mayonaise

1 teaspoon kimchi brine

2 slices bacon

2 large eggs

¼ teaspoon Diamond Crystal kosher salt

1½ teaspoons butter

2 tablespoons chopped kimchi, drained

2 slices American cheese

½ avocado, sliced

Toast the English muffins until golden brown. Set aside.

In a small bowl, whisk together the mayo and kimchi brine. Set aside.

Heat a skillet over medium, add the bacon, and cook until crisp, about 5 minutes. Flip and cook until browned, about 5 more minutes. Transfer to a paper towel-lined plate.

While the bacon is cooking, break the eggs into a small mixing bowl and season with the salt. Whisk until no whites remain.

Heat a skillet over medium heat, add the butter, and let it melt. Once the butter is frothy, add the eggs and cook, agitating continuously with a spatula, for about 1 to 2 minutes, or until just set.

Layer the chopped kimchi onto the bottoms of each muffin, and top with the scrambled eggs.

Add a slice of American cheese over each, then transfer to a toaster oven and cook at 350°F (175°C) until the cheese is melted, about 1 minute. (You can also do this in a preheated oven.)

Remove from the toaster oven, and top with the sliced avocado and bacon. Spread the mayo mixture over the tops of the muffins and close the sandwich. Serve immediately.

Cheddar and Jalapeño Corn Spoonbread

SERVES 6 TO 8

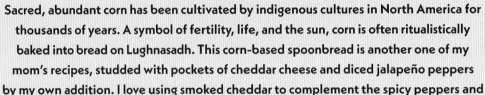

Sacred, abundant corn has been cultivated by indigenous cultures in North America for thousands of years. A symbol of fertility, life, and the sun, corn is often ritualistically baked into bread on Lughnasadh. This corn-based spoonbread is another one of my mom's recipes, studded with pockets of cheddar cheese and diced jalapeño peppers by my own addition. I love using smoked cheddar to complement the spicy peppers and sweet cornmeal, but you can also use regular cheddar. Serve with a sidecar of Hot Honey Butter (page 184) and a cold glass of Lemon Blueberry Radler (page 190).

1¼ cups (160 g) all-purpose flour

¾ cup (255 g) cornmeal

⅓ cup (70 g) granulated sugar

1 tablespoon baking powder

½ teaspoon Diamond Crystal kosher salt

1 jalapeño, seeded, ribs removed, and diced

4 ounces (115 g) freshly shredded cheddar, smoked or regular

2 large eggs

1 cup (240 ml) whole milk

¼ cup (60 ml) heavy whipping cream, plus an extra teaspoon or two for drizzling

¼ cup (60 ml) olive oil

Preheat the oven to 400°F (200°C). Grease a 9 x 9-inch (22 x 22-cm) pan and set aside.

In a large bowl, whisk together the flour, cornmeal, sugar, baking powder, and salt. Add the jalapeño and cheddar, reserving a handful of cheese to sprinkle on top. Stir to combine, then make a little well in the center of the mixture.

In a separate bowl, lightly beat the eggs. Add the milk, cream, and oil, then whisk to combine. Pour the wet ingredients into the dry ingredients, then fold them together very gently. Do NOT overstir!

Scrape the batter into the prepared pan and pour a little bit of cream on top in a swirl. Sprinkle the reserved cheddar over the top. Bake until set, 20 to 23 minutes. Test for doneness by inserting a butter knife in the center and making sure it comes out clean. Let cool for 10 minutes, then cut into squares.

Notes

- If you don't have a 9 x 9-inch pan, you can also use an 8 x 8-inch. Just add a couple minutes to the baking time.

- Don't overstir. When combining the dry and wet ingredients, use as few strokes as possible. Don't worry if there are a few little lumps.

- This cornbread is best eaten hot from the oven, but it will keep for a day or two when stored in an airtight container.

The best part about panzanella is that, unlike most salads, it tastes better the longer it sits. I recommend letting it marinate for two to six hours before serving. That means you can make it in the morning, before your kitchen gets too hot.

Bread Cheese Panzanella

SERVES 4 TO 6

Panzanella is a salad of chopped fresh vegetables and bread soaked in a flavorful dressing. Originally created as a way to use up stale bread, it's the perfect salad for celebrating the wheat harvest and the influx of juicy tomatoes and crisp cucumbers. My spin on the classic Italian salad includes bright fennel and, perhaps most importantly, cubes of bread cheese, a squeaky baked cheese similar to Halloumi. If you can't find bread cheese, you can sub in Halloumi or cheese curds. You can also skip the warm cheese aspect and use torn fresh mozzarella or cubed feta. Be sure to use stale bread so it can really soak up the dressing and tomato juice drippings. You can let the slices sit out overnight, or lightly toast them to dry them out. Pair with Pinot Grigio or the Raspberry Shrub Sparkler (page 189).

Four thick slices of slightly stale ciabatta

2 tablespoons olive oil

1 teaspoon Diamond Crystal kosher salt

½ red onion

2 tablespoons red wine vinegar, divided

1 tablespoon balsamic vinegar

1 teaspoon honey, spicy or plain

⅓ cup (80 ml) extra-virgin olive oil, plus 1 teaspoon

1 pound (455 g) heirloom tomatoes (about 3 medium-sized)

1 medium cucumber

½ small fennel bulb

¼ cup (16 g) fresh basil leaves

10 ounces (280 g) bread cheese

Kosher salt and freshly ground black pepper

Flaky salt, to serve

Preheat the oven to 400°F (200°C). Cut or tear the bread slices into roughly 1-inch (2.5-cm) cubes. Place on a baking sheet and toss with 2 tablespoons of olive oil and a teaspoon of kosher salt. Spread out and bake until toasted and golden, about 10 minutes. Make sure to flip the croutons halfway through. Let cool.

Meanwhile, thinly slice the onion into half-moons and place in a medium bowl. Cover with 1 tablespoon of red wine vinegar. Stir to combine and let macerate for about 20 minutes.

Remove onions and set aside. Whisk the red wine vinegar together with the balsamic and honey. Slowly whisk in ⅓ cup (80 ml) of the extra-virgin olive oil until emulsified. Set the dressing aside.

Cut the tomatoes into wedges, then cut the wedges in half. Set aside.

Quarter the cucumber lengthwise, then cut into ½-inch (1.25-cm) slices. Set aside.

(continued on page 176)

BREAD CHEESE PANZANELLA, *continued*

Cut the stalks and fronds off the fennel bulb and set aside. Slice the bulb in half, cut out the core, and discard. Thinly slice the bulb from top to bottom. Remove about a tablespoon of the fronds, and discard the rest. Thinly slice the stalks and finely chop the reserved fronds. Set aside.

Tear or roughly chop the basil. Set aside.

Put the cooled croutons in the bottom of a large salad bowl. Pour a few tablespoons of dressing over the croutons and toss to combine.

Put the tomatoes on top of the croutons, and sprinkle with a pinch of salt. Let sit for 10 minutes, so the juices drip over the croutons.

Meanwhile, prep the bread cheese. Heat a nonstick skillet over medium-low and drizzle in about a teaspoon of extra-virgin olive oil. Cut the bread cheese into 1-inch cubes. When the oil starts to shimmer, add the cubes to the pan. Let cook until browned, about 5 minutes. Flip and continue to cook until browned and pudgy on the sides, about 5 more minutes. Remove from the pan and let cool for 5 minutes, while you prep the rest of the salad.

Add the cucumbers, sliced fennel, and red onion to the salad bowl. Drizzle the remaining salad dressing over everything. Season to taste with a sprinkle of kosher salt and black pepper. Gently toss to combine.

Add the bread cheese cubes, and gently toss. Cover and let sit in the fridge for at least an hour. Finish with the basil, chopped fennel fronds, and a sprinkle of flaky salt just before serving.

Note

If making the salad ahead of time, store it in the fridge in an airtight container for up to 2 days. Reserve the basil and fennel fronds, and add just before serving.

On Bread Cheese

Bread cheese has the look and feel of a piece of baked Halloumi. Originally from Finland, where they call her leipäjuusto or juustoleipä, she's traditionally made with reindeer milk, but cow's milk is much more common nowadays. She's created by pressing cheese curds into a slab, then baking until the surface caramelizes and forms a toasty crust. Her texture is smooth and bouncy at room temperature, but the real magic happens when you get her hot on a grill or skillet. Like Halloumi, she doesn't lose her shape when heated but softens into a more luscious version of herself. She's mild and milky like cheese curds, but with a mouth-filling, buttery flavor and toasty notes. She's traditionally served slathered with jam like a slice of toast alongside a hot cup of coffee. I also love her with a drizzle of maple syrup and fresh summer berries.

Lemon Pizza with Pesto, Prosciutto, and Smoked Gouda

SERVES 2 TO 3

This unexpected combination of ingredients is my all-time favorite pizza. It's my mom's recipe, heavily adapted from one she cut out of an issue of *Parade* magazine years ago. My mom makes hers with smoked mozzarella, but I use Gouda. I love how the sweetness of the cheese complements the honey and contrasts with the salty flavors of other toppings. You can use either cheese here: just remember to check the label to make sure the cheese is physically smoked rather than flavored with overpowering liquid smoke. Pair with a chilled red like Lambrusco, a pilsner, or a glass of Orange Blossom Lemonade (page 160).

All-purpose flour, for dusting

1 pound (455 g) pizza dough (store-bought or homemade)

Semolina or cornmeal, for sprinkling

⅓ cup (60 g) Kath's Famous Pesto (page 155)

8 ounces (225 g) smoked Gouda or smoked mozzarella, freshly shredded

1 small lemon

Pinch of kosher salt (preferably Diamond Crystal)

2 tablespoons honey (I use the Hot Honey on page 130, but you can use any kind you'd like.)

¼ to ½ teaspoon red pepper flakes

3 slices prosciutto, torn into pieces

Preheat the oven to 500°F (260°C).

Dust your work surface with a couple of teaspoons of flour and roll out your pizza dough to fit inside a half-sheet pan. Let it rest for about 15 minutes and reroll if it shrinks.

Sprinkle the baking sheet with a couple of teaspoons of semolina or cornmeal and gently set the pizza dough on top. Spread the pesto over the dough, leaving about a ½-inch (1.2-cm) border. Sprinkle with the cheese.

Slice the lemon as thinly as possible, preferably using a mandolin. Discard the ends and remove the seeds. Scatter over the cheese and season each slice with a little salt.

Generously drizzle the honey over the pizza, being careful to avoid the crust. Sprinkle with the red pepper flakes, and finish with the prosciutto.

Bake in the oven until the crust is browning slightly and the cheese is melted and golden, about 10 to 12 minutes. Cool for 5 minutes, then slice and serve with extra honey on the side.

A Gift of the Ancients

The perfect canvas for all of the season's ripening fruits, cheesecake has roots as a harvest food. Cheese-based cakes date back to at least 234 BC, when ancient Greeks served them as bloodless sacrifices to the gods, in the hopes of ensuring an abundant crop. The first cheesecake recipe was published around 160 BC in *De agri cultura*. Written by Marcus Porcius Cato, the famed Roman agricultural manual also detailed recipes for cheese soufflés, puddings, and placenta cakes, which sound gross but were actually just huge pastries filled with about 14 pounds of cheese and nearly 5 pounds of honey.

Goat Cheesecake with Honey Tea–Poached Peaches

MAKES 1 CHEESECAKE

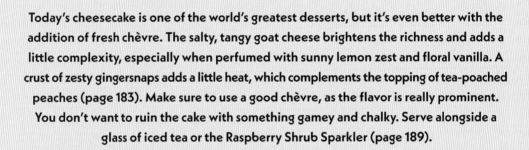

Today's cheesecake is one of the world's greatest desserts, but it's even better with the addition of fresh chèvre. The salty, tangy goat cheese brightens the richness and adds a little complexity, especially when perfumed with sunny lemon zest and floral vanilla. A crust of zesty gingersnaps adds a little heat, which complements the topping of tea-poached peaches (page 183). Make sure to use a good chèvre, as the flavor is really prominent. You don't want to ruin the cake with something gamey and chalky. Serve alongside a glass of iced tea or the Raspberry Shrub Sparkler (page 189).

FOR THE CRUST

9 ounces (255 g) gingersnaps

2 tablespoons granulated sugar

¼ teaspoon Diamond Crystal kosher salt

6 tablespoons unsalted butter, melted

FOR THE FILLING

16 ounces (340 g) fresh chèvre, at room temperature

8 ounces (170 g) cream cheese

¾ cup (150 g) granulated sugar

¼ teaspoon Diamond Crystal kosher salt

1 tablespoon lemon zest

2 large eggs

1 teaspoon vanilla extract

Make the crust: Preheat the oven to 350°F (175°C).

Place the cookies in the bowl of a food processor and pulse until they resemble sand. Add the sugar and salt and pulse again to combine. Pour in the melted butter and pulse until the mixture is thoroughly moistened.

Press the mixture into the bottom of a 10-inch (23-cm) springform pan. Use a glass or measuring cup with a flat bottom to ensure the mixture is spread evenly.

Bake until the crust is slightly browned, about 12 to 14 minutes. Let cool completely.

Make the filling: Preheat the oven to 400°F (200°C).

In a large bowl, use an electric mixer to gently beat together the chévre, cream cheese, sugar, salt, and lemon zest until smooth.

(continued on page 182)

GOAT CHEESECAKE WITH HONEY TEA-POACHED PEACHES, *continued*

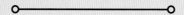

In a separate small mixing bowl, beat the eggs with the vanilla. Pour the egg mixture into the cheese mixture and mix on low speed to combine. Pour the filling into the crust.

Bake until the edges are golden but the center is still jiggly, about 22 to 24 minutes. Remove from the oven and cool to room temperature. If storing for later, cool completely (about 3 hours) before transferring to the fridge.

When ready to serve, top with the Honey Tea-Poached Peaches (opposite page).

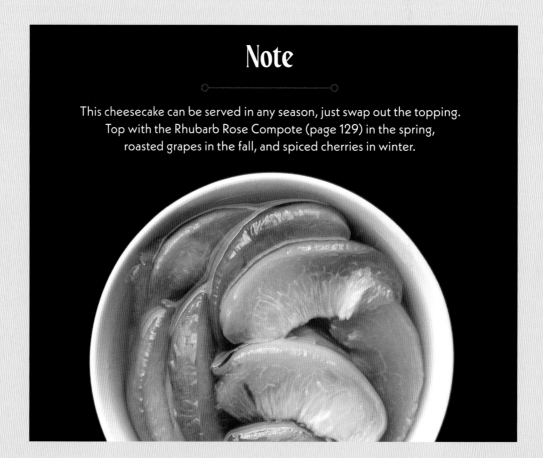

Note

This cheesecake can be served in any season, just swap out the topping. Top with the Rhubarb Rose Compote (page 129) in the spring, roasted grapes in the fall, and spiced cherries in winter.

Honey Tea-Poached Peaches

MAKES 12 OUNCES (340 G) OF POACHED PEACHES

Honey and chamomile emphasize the delicate sweet flavors of summer's favorite stone fruit. Make sure to use firm peaches for this recipe. They should still easily pull away from the pit, but if they're too ripe, they'll get mushy when poached. Serve the honeyed peaches with creamy blue cheeses or over Goat Cheesecake (page 181).

2 tablespoons chamomile tea (about 6 bags)

⅔ cup (135 g) granulated sugar

2 cups (290 g) sliced peaches (about 2 to 3 peaches)

¼ cup (60 ml) honey

1 tablespoon freshly squeezed lemon juice (about half a lemon)

¼ teaspoon Diamond Crystal kosher salt

Fill a medium saucepan with 1 cup (240 ml) of water and bring to a boil. Put the chamomile into tea bags or a strainer.

Turn off the heat and add the chamomile to the water. Cover and steep for 15 minutes.

Remove the tea bags or strainer and bring back to a simmer. Stir in the sugar and cook until fully dissolved, about 3 minutes.

Add the sliced peaches and cook until tender but not mushy, about 6 to 8 minutes. Remove from the heat and let cool for about 5 minutes. Stir in the honey, lemon juice, and salt.

Transfer to a 12-ounce mason jar, cover, and store in the fridge for about 2 weeks.

Peaches are native to China, and according to ancient Taoist folklore, they're associated with the goddess Xiwangmu. Known as the Queen Mother of the West, Xiwangmu lives in a sacred garden with a tree bearing celestial peaches that would grant immortality to whoever ate them but only ripened every 3,000 years. Today, peaches are considered a symbol of fertility and longevity.

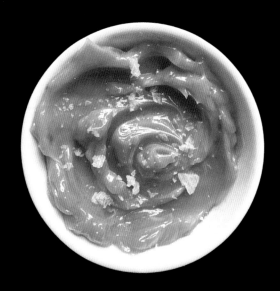

Hot Honey Butter

MAKES 4 OUNCES (115 G)

Honey is the nectar of the gods and a potent symbol of the sun, especially when enriched with spicy chilis. Since butter symbolizes the moon, whipping both of these magical ingredients together balances their potent energies and creates an enchanting accompaniment for breads and bakes. If you're using homemade spicy honey, be sure to strain out any chilis to avoid compromising the texture of the butter. Serve with Cheddar and Jalapeño Corn Spoonbread (page 172).

½ cup (115 g) unsalted butter, at room temperature

3 tablespoons Hot Honey (page 130)

⅛ to ¼ teaspoon Diamond Crystal kosher salt

Flaky salt, to taste

Place the butter in a medium mixing bowl. Add the honey and salt, then whisk until incorporated. Taste for salt and add flaky salt to taste. Refrigerate in an airtight container, where it will keep for 7 to 10 days.

Corn Ceremonies

People have cultivated corn throughout the southern regions of North America for at least 7,000 years. Kernels were cooked into stews or milled and baked into bread, their husks dried and woven into baskets. Many people celebrated the arrival of this precious crop with Green Corn Ceremonies. The individual traditions varied across tribes, but the rituals celebrated new beginnings and gave thanks for the harvest with sacred fires, fasting, and feasting. In some practices, the verdant first crop was sacrificed to the gods in hopes of a healthy and abundant harvest.

Today, many modern pagans honor the goddesses of the harvest with the ancient tradition of making corn dollies from the dried husks. Sometimes they bury the dolls at Imbolc to fertilize the ground. Others ritualistically "sacrifice" the doll by burning it, feeding it to animals, or burying it in the fields to ensure crops for the following year.

Grilled Marinated Eggplant

SERVES 4 TO 6

A member of the nightshade family, the aubergine is a symbol of abundance and fertility that's often featured in divination rituals, protection spells, and money magic. Flavored with garlic and rosemary to boost its protective qualities, mint to amplify the powers of abundance, and capers to enhance the fertile energies, these grilled nightshades taste incredible on pasta showered with Parm, with ciabatta and burrata, or alongside the cheeses on the Money Spell Plate (page 196).

1 pound (455 g) eggplant

½ teaspoon kosher salt (preferably Diamond Crystal), divided

¼ cup (60 ml) olive oil

2 garlic cloves, minced

1 tablespoon chopped fresh rosemary

3 tablespoons chopped fresh mint, divided

2 tablespoons capers, drained and roughly chopped

¼ teaspoon freshly ground black pepper

Balsamic vinegar, for drizzling

Cut the eggplant into ½-inch (1.2-cm) slices, then spread out on a cutting board. Season with ¼ teaspoon of salt. Let sit until the beads of moisture pool on the surface, about 10 minutes. Flip and repeat on the other side.

Transfer to a colander and rinse under cool water. Use a clean dish towel or paper towels to dry off the slices. Set aside.

In a medium bowl, mix the olive oil with the garlic, rosemary, 2 tablespoons of mint, capers, and black pepper. Toss the eggplant in the marinade, making sure both sides are coated.

Heat your grill to medium, about 450°F (230°C).

Shake off the marinade and arrange the eggplant on the grill.

Grill until nicely charred, about 6 minutes. Then flip and grill until soft and toasty on both sides, another 6 minutes.

Return the eggplant to the marinade and let cool. Arrange on a serving dish, drizzle with the balsamic vinegar, sprinkle with the remaining mint, and serve.

Note

If you're not serving immediately,
then store in an airtight container in
the refrigerator for 7 to 10 days.
Bring to room temperature and
garnish before serving.

What's a Shrub?

The shrub has held many meanings throughout history, but in general, it is a method of preserving fruits by using vinegar and sugar to transform them into a drinkable potion. You can make a shrub with almost any fruit, and some even use vegetables.

If you're not interested in waiting over a week for your shrub, you can make a quick version. Add a cup of water and a cup of sugar to a small saucepan and heat over low until the sugar dissolves. Add the fruit and cook for about 10 minutes, until the juices extract from the fruit. Strain out the solids, add the vinegars, transfer to a bottle, and store in the refrigerator for up to 6 months.

Raspberry Shrub Sparkler

MAKES 1 COCKTAIL

One of my most precious childhood memories is of picking raspberries with my grandmother in my grandfather's garden. Perhaps this recipe is an attempt to preserve that experience, in addition to saving these ruby-red jewels of summer. This shrub is cold-processed, which protects the fresh, bright flavors of the fruit but also takes a really long time. It's ready to drink in a week but tastes best after two or three. Pair with ricotta and shortbread or with the Lughnasadh Plate (page 192).

FOR THE SHRUB
(makes about 16 ounces/ 480 ml)

2 cups (250 g) fresh raspberries, washed

1 cup (200 g) granulated sugar

½ cup (120 ml) cider vinegar

½ cup (120 ml) champagne vinegar

FOR THE SPARKLER

1 ounce (60 ml) shrub

4 to 6 ounces (240 to 360 ml) seltzer

1 lime wedge

1 lime wheel, to garnish

Fresh mint sprig, to garnish

Make the shrub: Add the raspberries and sugar to a medium bowl. Stir until the fruit is covered in sugar, crushing the berries with a spoon. Cover and store in the fridge until the fruit is surrounded by juices, at least 6 hours and up to 2 days.

Set a fine-mesh strainer over a measuring cup. Pour the mixture through, pressing the fruit to fully release all the juices and scraping any sugar left in the bowl into the syrup.

Pour the vinegars over the solids into the syrup to rinse off any remaining sugars. Discard the solids.

Whisk the shrub together, and transfer to a bottle or mason jar. Close the bottle, label with the date, and store in the fridge until the sugar dissolves, about 1 week. The longer the shrub sits, the more mellow it will become. I like it best around 3 weeks, but it will stay good for at least 6 months and sometimes even a year.

Make the cocktail: Fill a glass with ice and add the shrub and seltzer. Squeeze the lime wedge into the glass. Stir to combine and garnish with a lime wheel and a mint sprig.

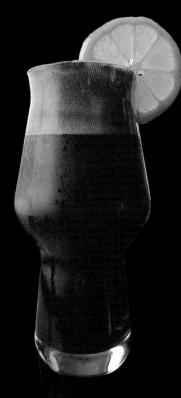

Lemon Blueberry Radler

MAKES 1 COCKTAIL

My take on the classic German cocktail features tart blueberry syrup. The abundant, antioxidant-rich berries are cooked down into a syrup and stirred with freshly squeezed lemon juice and crisp lager, a bright tonic that tastes like the dog days of summer while refreshing you from the oppressive heat. Pair with the Lughnasadh Plate (page 192) or fresh chèvre and a baguette.

FOR THE BLUEBERRY SYRUP
(makes 12 ounces/355 ml)

¾ cup (150 g) granulated sugar

1 tablespoon lemon zest (about 1 lemon)

10 ounces (285 g) fresh blueberries

FOR THE RADLER

1 ounce (30 ml) freshly squeezed lemon juice

2 ounces (60 ml) blueberry syrup

12 ounces (355 ml) kölsch, wheat beer, pilsner, or mild lager

1 lemon wheel, to garnish

Make the syrup: Add the sugar and lemon zest to a medium bowl and rub together with your fingers until sandy and fragrant. Transfer to a small saucepan. Add the blueberries and ½ cup (120 ml) of water. Heat over low and cook until the berries release their juices and the sugar dissolves, about 10 minutes. Use a wooden spoon to smash the berries. Let cool for about 5 minutes, and then strain out the solids. The syrup will keep for about 10 days in an airtight container in the fridge.

Make the cocktail: Add the lemon juice and blueberry syrup to a pint glass. Pour in the beer at an angle and stir until combined. Garnish with the lemon wheel and serve.

Lugh, the Celtic Sun God

This late-summer festival honors Lugh, a warrior god of the harvest whose name means "the shining one." According to Irish mythology, he's the king of the Tuatha Dé Danann, a sacred race known as the tribe of gods. As a child, Lugh was saved and adopted by the mortal queen Tailtiu. After she died, he dedicated his festival to her as part of her funeral ceremony. Lughnasadh dates back to at least 1600 BC, and was originally celebrated with feasting, horse races, and even sword fights.

1   La Tur

is a cupcake-shaped cheese from Caseificio dell'Alta Langa in Italy that's made with three different milk types: grassy goat, buttery cow, and nutty sheep. The magical trio creates a silky yet fluffy texture with a sweet milky tang and a delicate, wrinkled rind that smells of freshly baked bread. Spread onto a piece of baguette and top with a slice of Honey Tea-Poached Peach.

2   Grayson

is an iconically stinky raw milk washed rind from Meadow Creek Dairy in Galax, Virginia. She's only made when the farm's herd of Jersey cows is out to pasture, so each wheel is infused with the magic of an Appalachian pasture in bloom. She tastes like custard, bacon, and garlic, and has a plush, bouncy texture. Pair her with a blackberry—the brambly notes complement her brothy flavors.

3   Le Gruyère AOP

is an enchanting Alpine goddess and Switzerland's most popular cheese. Most of us first encounter her bubbling over French onion soup or melting sensually into fondue, but she also shines on a cheese plate. Pair a thin slice with a cherry and a cracker.

4   Bleu d'Auvergne

is essentially the cow's milk version of Roquefort, but she's much more mellow than her sheep's milk sister. She's soft and spreadable with a slightly spicy bite that sparkles with a little pepper jelly and a sweet corn cookie.

FRESH BAGUETTE

honors the ritual of baking in celebration of the grain harvest.

PEACHES

Peaches are the epitome of high summer, especially when poached in a syrup of chamomile and honey (page 183).

BLACKBERRIES

are traditionally eaten during harvest festivals and offer a rich, deep flavor that plays off the meaty notes in washed rind cheeses.

PROSCIUTTO-WRAPPED MELON

Ancient Romans believed cantaloupe and cured meat was an immune-boosting snack, and today prosciutto-wrapped melon is a rejuvenating summertime staple.

PEPPER JELLY

contrasts with the
salty cheeses.

CORN BISCUITS

provide a sweet, crunchy
bed for the creamy blue.

**FRUIT AND
NUT CRISPS**

tease out the toasty
notes in the Gruyère.

CHERRIES

pair with all the cheeses,
but their sweet juice is
especially rewarding
with the earthy blue.

THE LUGHNA-SADH PLATE

Bejeweled with the fruits of the season, the
Lughnasadh Plate celebrates the first
harvest with a trio of carbs: fresh baguette,
sweet corn biscuits, and fig-studded
crackers. The earth is exploding with a
seemingly infinite bounty, and all we can do
is pair it with cheese. The featured four are
some of my favorites to pair with an abundant feast of berries, melon, and stone fruit.
Pour yourself a Raspberry Shrub Sparkler
(page 189) and enjoy the final days of
sunlight before autumn's arrival.

Blackberries and Michaelmas

According to old Christian folklore, it's
forbidden to harvest blackberries after
Michaelmas, which falls near the autumnal
equinox on September 29. Legend has it
that this was the day that the Archangel
Michael slayed Satan, who fell into a
blackberry bush. In a fury, the devil
trampled the brambles and vandalized
the bush with his bodily fluids, thus
cursing the berries left on the branches.

THE CONSERVAS PLATE

When the sun is strong and the humidity is thick, turning on your oven or stove feels like an actual gateway to hell. It's simply too hot to cook. Instead, I find myself craving a platter filled with little tins of oily fishes served alongside cheeses, pickles, and crunchy crackers. While the practice of preserving fish in tins or jars dates back to late eighteenth-century France, it's the Iberian Peninsula that made these conservas so popular. During the two world wars, Portugal expanded its tinned sardine production to feed the troops. The industry continued to thrive long after the wars ended, and Portugal is now known as the conservas capital to this day. Tinned fish is produced all over the world, from Japan to Alaska, and comes in a dazzling array of variations. I've featured two of my favorites in this platter, but please feel free to swap them out for whatever speaks to you. Pair with sparkling wine, a lemon-infused seltzer on the rocks, or an ice-cold Perfect Martini with a blue cheese olive (page 216).

POTATO CHIPS
are a classic pairing with conservas, best used as a salty base for the fish (à la a sea nacho).

FLATBREAD CRACKERS
are perfect for building bites of creamy cheeses and briny fish or for dipping into the flavorful oils.

CUCUMBER SLICES
act as both a vehicle for toppings and a fresh, crisp palate cleanser.

OCTOPUS
has an especially tender texture when prepared for conservas, especially when it's slow cooked in smoky, paprika-spiked Galician sauce.

SARDINES

come packed in a wide array of flavored oils, but the sunny, lemon-infused variety is a personal favorite of mine.

2

1

1 Meredith Dairy Marinated Sheep & Goat Cheese

consists of fluffy, cloudlike cubes bathed in a garlic, herb, and peppercorn-infused oil. Founded in 1991, Meredith Dairy is a sustainable farmstead creamery in Victoria, Australia, that makes yogurt and fresh cheese from the milk of their herds of sheep and goats. The marinated cheese is so enchanting that she goes by "Aussie Magic" at the Cheese Shop of Salem, in Massachusetts. Spread her onto flatbread and pair it with sardines and a squirt of lemon.

2 Zamorano

is made with the raw milk of the local Churra and Castellana sheep in the Castile and León regions of the Spanish Zamora province. At first glance, she resembles Manchego and has a similarly nutty flavor. Her iconic spicy finish sets her apart, though, flooding your palate with buttery almond notes before leaving the tip of your tongue sizzling with piquancy. Pair with Gildas or octopus in Galician sauce.

GILDAS

are a briny Spanish appetizer consisting of anchovies, green peppers, and olives on a skewer.

LEMON WEDGES

add acidity to cut through all the rich, oil-soaked conservas.

FENNEL

brings a bright, licorice flavor that tastes divine when drizzled with the herbaceous oil from the marinated cheese.

1 Quadrello di Bufala

Quadrello di Bufala is a washed rind cheese with a funky, mushroom flavor that's similar to Taleggio but made with the milk of water buffalo. With twice the fat of cow's milk, the resulting cheese has a mouth-filling richness that begs for a little acidity. Pair with the tomatoes or the briny eggplant.

2 Pecorino Toscano

is made with sheep's milk, which has double the solids of cow's milk. While the extra fat and protein equate to more cheesemaking potential, ewes also produce a lot less compared to bovines. This means what they make is very precious (i.e., expensive), but also transforms into rich, luxurious cheeses. Buy a wedge of nutty Pecorino Toscano and slice it into eight pieces, the number associated with financial success. Plate next to the honey and cashews.

3 Colston Bassett Stilton

is made with hand-ladled curds, creating a tender texture that crumbles like a buttery biscuit. She's both salty and sweet with a cave-like musk and long finish that unfolds into notes of smoky bacon and milk chocolate fudge. If you can't find her, try Bayley Hazen Blue from Jasper Hill Farm in Vermont or even Italian Gorgonzola. Pair with flaxseed crackers and dates.

TOMATOES are plentiful in the summertime and are a potent money attractor, especially when paired with eggplant and basil.

BASIL is associated with fiery Mars energy and is one of the most common ingredients in money spells.

CASHEWS bring out the Pecorino's nutty notes and are commonly used to manifest financial gain.

(page 186) is associated with prosperity, especially when it's grilled, marinated in luscious olive oil, and paired with buttery Quadrello.

FLAXSEED
CRACKERS

are a potent money attractor, and the crackers represent the grain harvest.

THE MONEY SPELL PLATE

This season of bounty is an apt time to work some money magic with an indulgent cheese platter. I highly recommend building this plate on a Thursday, the day lucky of Jupiter, while the moon is in her waxing phase. Cleanse your space before you start, then set out your ingredients and thank all the flora, fauna, and human beings who brought them to your table. The most effective money spells always start with gratitude. Put the plate together, while envisioning money flowing to you. Once you're done, recite the spell below three times. Then pour yourself a glass of Lemon Blueberry Radler (page 190), toast to the harvest, and consume while envisioning that coin coming your way.

Money Spell

Before indulging in the plate, take a moment to give thanks to all who brought these blessings to you. Then repeat this invocation three times:

Powerful harvest, bring me wealth
Blessings of prosperity
To no one's harm of soul or health
This I ask, so mote it be
As above, so below
Money, money come to me

3

DATES

are associated with Jupiter, according to Vedic astrology, which is the planet of expansion and money magic.

HONEY

offers solar-powered sweetness to attract funds.

MABON

Just like Ostara, the autumnal equinox marks the moment when nature hangs in perfect balance. The days are the same length as the nights. This time, however, we look toward the waxing darkness, turning inward and readying our bodies and homes for the winter as the sun's reign ends. Meanwhile, we are surrounded by the opulent bounty of the harvest: all we planted in spring has grown, fruited, and ripened. This is the Witch's Thanksgiving, a festival of abundance, recognition for all you've accomplished, and gratitude for plentiful nourishment and all those who work to bring it to you. Mabon is also a time to prepare for the coming winter, preserving the plenty and taking stock of what we need to survive the cold, barren months.

Fontina Val d'Aosta

○────────────────○

While there are a ton of imitations out
there, I highly recommend tracking down
Fontina Val d'Aosta from Italy. Fontinella
and Fontina are milky sweet and plenty
meltable, but they've got nothing on the
plum and mushroom notes of the real
thing. She's a fantastic breakfast cheese,
especially when melted over braised
kale and topped with a fried egg
and pickled shallots.

Braised Kale and Fontina Tartine

MAKES 2 TARTINES

Native to the Mediterranean and Middle East, kale is a descendant of wild cabbage that has been cultivated for at least 4,500 years. One of my favorite ways to cook it is with a quick braise. I love how the pile of rugged leaves melts down, soaking up all of that flavorful broth and transforming from bitter cruciferous stalk into a tender, velvety bed just waiting for melted fontina. Serve with black coffee or oolong tea.

1½ tablespoons butter, divided

½ shallot, thinly sliced

1 bunch (about 8 ounces/ 200 g) lacinato kale, stems removed and roughly chopped

¾ cup (180 ml) broth (beef, mushroom, or chicken works best)

2 slices sourdough, sliced 1 inch thick

2 ounces (55 g) fontina, at room temperature and freshly shredded

2 large eggs

Diamond Crystal kosher salt

1 tablespoon Pickled Shallots (page 210), drained and roughly chopped

Freshly ground black pepper

Flaky salt

Heat a skillet over medium-low. Add 1 tablespoon of butter and let it melt. Once it's frothy, add the sliced shallots and cook until fragrant and soft, about 5 minutes. Add the kale and stir to coat in the butter.

Pour the broth over the kale. Stir to combine, then cover with a lid. Cook for 5 minutes, stirring halfway through.

Remove the lid, increase heat to medium, and cook, stirring occasionally, until the liquid evaporates, about 10 more minutes.

While the kale cooks, lightly toast the sourdough until golden brown and crunchy.

Arrange a small bed of kale atop each slice of sourdough. Evenly distribute the fontina over the kale. Transfer to a toaster oven or broiler and cook until the cheese melts, about 1 to 2 minutes.

Meanwhile, wipe out the skillet and heat over medium. Add the remaining ½ tablespoon of butter and swirl around the pan. Add the eggs and season with salt. Cook for 1 minute. Cover with a lid and let cook until set, about 1 to 2 minutes.

Slide an egg onto each toast. Sprinkle with the pickled shallots and finish with black pepper and flaky salt.

Pesto-Baked Camembert with Roasted Grapes

SERVES 2 TO 4

I first encountered the combination of pesto and grapes on a sandwich at my favorite restaurant, Lula Cafe in Chicago. I loved how the bright, garlicky sauce coated the fruit, teasing out her earthy notes and taming her sweetness. But it was the palette that bewitched me. Those flecks of rich green coating the deep purple orbs, glimmering with olive oil—fall fashion on focaccia. There's a lot happening here, so I recommend a French-made Camembert. They're more robust than Brie, with earthy, allium-forward notes that can stand up to the pesto. If you want to dive deeper into the funk and harvest colors, use an orange-hued washed rind cheese, like Taleggio or Willoughby from Jasper Hill Farm in Vermont. Serve with a seeded baguette and a bright red wine or a sparkling apple cider.

8-ounce (255 g) wheel of Camembert

Freshly ground black pepper

2 tablespoons pesto

¼ cup (75 g) Roasted Grapes (page 214)

Sliced seeded baguette

Bring the cheese to room temperature before baking. This ensures that it will heat evenly and won't separate.

Preheat the oven to 350°F (175°C). Use a sharp knife to score a crosshatch pattern into the top rind of the cheese. Don't go all the way to the bottom, though!

Place the Camembert inside a small baking dish or skillet, sprinkle a little black pepper over, and transfer to the oven. Bake for 10 minutes.

Remove from the oven. Spoon the pesto over the cheese and scatter the grapes on top. Return to the oven and bake for 5 more minutes.

Let cool for 5 minutes. Surround with a wreath of sliced baguette and serve immediately.

Vinaigrette

1 tablespoon Dijon mustard

2 tablespoons cider vinegar

2 teaspoons maple syrup

½ teaspoon Diamond Crystal kosher salt

¼ teaspoon freshly ground black pepper

½ cup (120 ml) extra-virgin olive oil

MAKES ABOUT ¾ CUP (180 ML)

Whisk together the mustard, vinegar, syrup, salt, and pepper until fully combined. Whisk in the oil until emulsified and thick. Store in an airtight container in the refrigerator for up to 2 weeks.

Cheddar Apple Salad

SERVES 4

This salad is as crisp as a perfect autumn day. Tart green apples are shocked with lemon water to prevent browning and complement their natural tang, then bedded onto crisp lettuce, and anointed with a cider-forward vinaigrette. Sweetened with candied pecans and brightened with pickled shallots, the crowning jewel is big crumbles of bandaged cheddar. While block cheddars are more common, cheddars that are wrapped in cloth before aging have an acidic bite and subtle, musty cave notes reminiscent of the darkness that closes in as the sun wanes and the moon waxes. Assemble the salad just before serving, lest the zippy dressing wilts the greens. Serve with a chilled glass of apple cider or malty IPA.

1 green apple, cored and thinly sliced

2 teaspoons freshly squeezed lemon juice

16 ounces (455 g) red or green leaf lettuce, washed and dried

¼ cup (60 ml) Vinaigrette (opposite)

Kosher salt

Freshly ground black pepper

2 tablespoons Pickled Shallots (page 210), chopped

2 tablespoons Bourbon-Glazed Pecans (page 213) chopped

3 ounces (85 g) bandaged cheddar, crumbled

Slice the apple in half, then cut out the core. Slice thinly.

In a small bowl, whisk the lemon juice with ½ cup (120 ml) of water. Add the apple slices and toss to coat. Let sit for a minute, then drain the water.

Add the lettuce to a large salad bowl and pour over the Vinaigrette, reserving a tablespoon for finishing. Toss to combine, and season with the salt and pepper. Toss again, taste a leaf for seasoning, and adjust as needed.

Transfer to a serving platter, and top with the apples. Drizzle with the remaining dressing. Finish with the shallots, pecans, cheddar, and more black pepper.

Stovetop Mac and Cheese

SERVES 2 TO 3

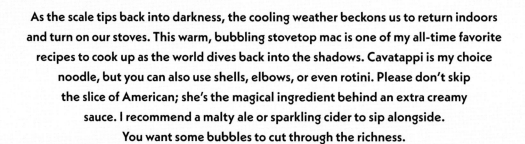

As the scale tips back into darkness, the cooling weather beckons us to return indoors and turn on our stoves. This warm, bubbling stovetop mac is one of my all-time favorite recipes to cook up as the world dives back into the shadows. Cavatappi is my choice noodle, but you can also use shells, elbows, or even rotini. Please don't skip the slice of American; she's the magical ingredient behind an extra creamy sauce. I recommend a malty ale or sparkling cider to sip alongside. You want some bubbles to cut through the richness.

Salt for the pasta water
½ pound (228 g) cavatappi pasta
1½ tablespoons butter
1½ tablespoons flour
1½ cups (600 ml) whole milk
¼ teaspoon garlic powder
¼ teaspoon smoked paprika
⅛ teaspoon cayenne
¼ teaspoon black pepper
½ teaspoon Diamond Crystal kosher salt
1 slice American cheese
8 ounces (170 g) cheddar

Fill a large pot with water, salt heavily, and bring to a boil over high heat. Add pasta and cook according to the package directions until al dente, stirring occasionally. Drain the pasta.

Melt the butter in a large saucepan over medium heat. Reduce to medium-low, sprinkle the flour into the mixture, and cook, whisking constantly, until toasty and golden, about 2 minutes.

In a liquid measuring cup, combine the milk, garlic powder, paprika, cayenne, black pepper, and kosher salt. Slowly pour it into the flour mixture, adding just a little at a time and whisking to incorporate after each addition.

Whisking constantly, bring to a low simmer. Cook, whisking occasionally, until thick and smooth, 6 minutes.

Remove from the heat, add the American cheese, and whisk until melted. Add the cheddar a handful at a time, whisking until melted after each addition. Pour the pasta into the sauce, and stir to combine. Serve immediately.

Pecorino Plum Crumble

SERVES 4

Like many fruits, plums are associated with Venus, and this warm, bubbling crumble is an altar to the Roman goddess. Oats, cardamom, and vanilla are all ruled by the planet of love, while the Pecorino Romano featured here dates back to the ancient city for which she's named. Plums and sheep's milk cheeses are a classic, no-fail pairing; They highlight each other's fruity notes while the Pecorino's salty nuttiness contrasts with the plum's sweetness. Pair it with a hot mug of coffee or glass of champagne.

1 pound (455 g) plums, pitted and sliced

1 vanilla bean or 2 teaspoons vanilla extract

3 tablespoons light brown sugar, divided

¼ teaspoon Diamond Crystal kosher salt

¼ cup (30 g) all-purpose flour

¾ cup (75 g) rolled oats

½ teaspoon ground cardamom

½ teaspoon cinnamon

¼ teaspoon ground cloves

1½ ounces (40 g) Pecorino Romano, finely grated

¼ cup unsalted butter, chopped

Vanilla ice cream, to serve

Preheat the oven to 350°F (175°C). Butter an 8-inch (20-cm) baking dish or skillet.

Place the plums in a medium mixing bowl. Scrape the seeds out of the vanilla bean and add to the plums with 1 tablespoon of the brown sugar, and ¼ teaspoon salt. Stir to combine, and transfer to the baking dish or skillet.

In a mixing bowl, combine the flour, oats, remaining brown sugar, cardamom, cinnamon, and cloves. Stir to incorporate, then add the butter and most of the cheese, reserving a little for topping. Use your hands to work it into the mixture so that crumbles form.

Spread the crumble over the plums in an even layer, and top with the remaining cheese. Bake for 40 minutes, until the top is golden brown and the plum juices are bubbling. Let cool for 10 minutes, then spoon onto plates and serve with a scoop of vanilla ice cream.

Pickled Shallots

MAKES 12 OUNCES (340 G)

Though we are surrounded by so much abundance at the harvest, there's a catch: all that plenty must make it through the winter. As squirrels gather nuts and bears fatten themselves, so too must we preserve our plenty. Obviously, grocery stores ensure our survival in any season, but the act of pickling still honors the autumnal ritual of preservation. Bathed in cider vinegar and perfumed with thyme, peppercorns, and a little garlic, these tangy pickled shallots add an acidic, oniony bite to any fall dish. Sprinkle over the Braised Kale and Fontina Tartine (page 201), toss into the Cheddar Apple Salad (page 205), or serve on the Mabon Cider Plate (page 218).

½ pound (230 g) shallots (about 4 to 5)

1 sprig fresh thyme

½ cup (120 ml) cider vinegar

½ cup (120 ml) water

1 tablespoon granulated sugar

1 tablespoon kosher salt

¼ teaspoon peppercorns

1 clove garlic, smashed

Peel the shallots, and trim off their roots. Slice into thin rings, and place inside a 12-ounce jar with the thyme.

Heat an enamel saucepan over medium. Add the vinegar, water, sugar, salt, peppercorns, and garlic and bring to a boil. Reduce the heat to a simmer and cook for 10 minutes, stirring occasionally.

Pour the brine over the shallots and let cool completely. Use a spoon to push the shallots down until they're fully submerged in the brine. Cover the jar and store it in the fridge for 24 hours. Pickled shallots will keep for about a month.

Pecorino Romano

Pecorino, meaning "of sheep" in Italian, is a category of sheep's milk cheeses that includes a wide variety of ages and textures. Named for her hometown of Rome, Pecorino Romano is firm, easy to grate, and salty enough to burn your tongue. She's a little intense on her own, but enchanting when shaved over salads or melted into cacio e pepe, which is essentially an Italian macaroni and cheese made with bucatini and lots of black pepper. According to the writings of Virgil and Marcus Porcius, Pecorino was a common ration for Roman soldiers. Bronze graters recently discovered in the graves of warrior princes date back to 900 BC, which suggests that Pecorinos might be at least that old. Sicilian soldiers of ancient Greece even drank an elixir that consisted of Sicilian cheeses grated directly into wine.

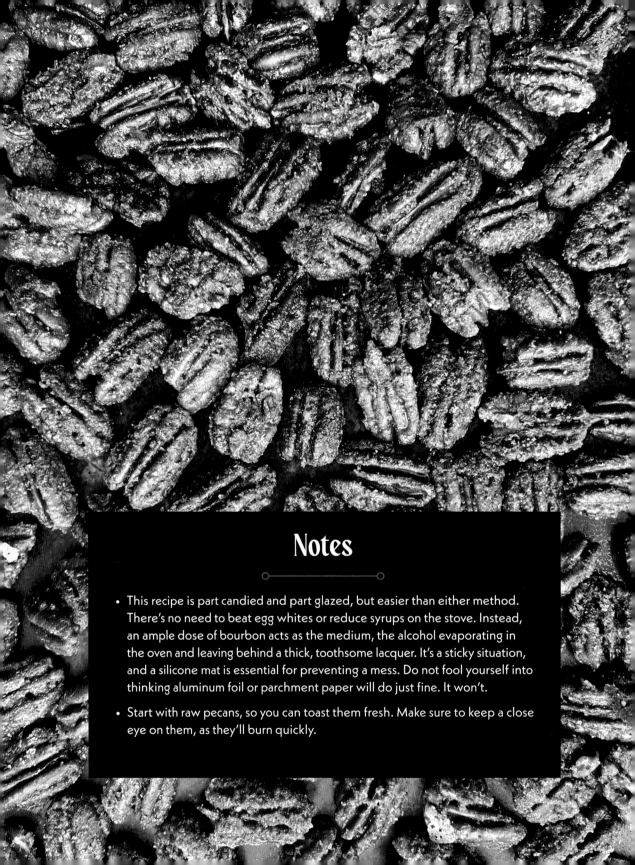

Notes

- This recipe is part candied and part glazed, but easier than either method. There's no need to beat egg whites or reduce syrups on the stove. Instead, an ample dose of bourbon acts as the medium, the alcohol evaporating in the oven and leaving behind a thick, toothsome lacquer. It's a sticky situation, and a silicone mat is essential for preventing a mess. Do not fool yourself into thinking aluminum foil or parchment paper will do just fine. It won't.

- Start with raw pecans, so you can toast them fresh. Make sure to keep a close eye on them, as they'll burn quickly.

Bourbon-Glazed Pecans

MAKES ABOUT 2 CUPS (200 G)

While they're available year-round, pecans ripen and fall from the trees in September. Their sweetness is a natural complement to baking spices, and I love how their ridges readily catch the seasonings. Pair with aged Gouda and fudgy blue cheeses or enjoy on the Cheddar Apple Salad (page 205).

- 2 cups (200 g) raw pecans
- ½ cup (100 g) brown light sugar
- ½ teaspoon cinnamon
- ¼ teaspoon ground cloves
- ¼ teaspoon ground black pepper
- ⅛ teaspoon cayenne pepper
- 1 teaspoon Diamond Crystal kosher salt
- 1 tablespoon unsalted butter, melted
- 2 tablespoons bourbon

Preheat the oven to 350°F (175°C). Line a baking sheet with a silicone mat.

Spread the nuts over the baking sheet, making an even layer. Don't pack them too tightly—you want to let them breathe a little.

Bake for 7 to 8 minutes, stirring halfway, until they smell fragrant and toasty. Remove from the oven and let cool slightly as you prepare the glaze.

In a medium mixing bowl, combine the sugar, cinnamon, cloves, black pepper, cayenne, and salt. Add the butter and bourbon and stir until incorporated.

Add the pecans to the bowl, and mix until thoroughly coated.

Spread the coated nuts onto the sheet pan and bake for about 8 minutes, stirring every few minutes to prevent burning and to keep the nuts coated. The glaze will look a little syrupy at first, but it will thicken fast.

Remove the nuts from the oven and let cool on the baking sheet until hard, about 10 minutes. When they're cool enough to touch, break up the clusters with your hands. Store in an airtight container for about 2 weeks.

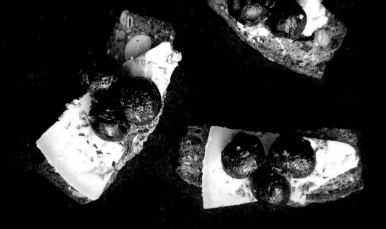

Roasted Grapes

MAKES ABOUT 1 CUP (150 G)

The autumnal equinox coincides with the grape harvest. At Mabon, vines are heavy with clusters of plump, ripened fruit, ready to adorn cheese plates or ferment into wine. Associated with wealth, abundance, and fertility deities like the Egyptian Hathor and the hedonistic Greek god Dionysus, grapes are lauded for their plentiful antioxidants and ability to transform into wine, an elixir of pleasure and joy. Roasting provides a preservation method that's much easier than winemaking, with a deep, robust flavor resulting in soft, jammy grapes. You can roast any grape, but I recommend seedless Concords if you can find them. Their flavor is so pronounced that it tastes almost artificial. Pair with caramel-sweet Norwegian brunost for a take on PB&J, spoon over Pesto-Baked Camembert (page 202), or serve on the Harvest Moon Plate (page 220).

2 cups (300 g) seedless Concord or red grapes

1 tablespoon peanut oil or other neutral cooking oil

½ teaspoon freshly squeezed lemon juice

2 teaspoons fresh rosemary leaves, chopped

¼ teaspoon salt

¼ teaspoon freshly ground black pepper

Preheat the oven to 425°F (220°C). Line a baking sheet with aluminum foil or a silicone mat.

Add the grapes to a medium mixing bowl and pour the oil and lemon juice over. Toss to coat, then sprinkle with the rosemary, salt, and pepper. Toss again until everything is evenly distributed.

Pour the grapes onto the baking sheet, transfer to the oven, and roast until the skins start to blister and the sugars caramelize, about 20 minutes. Let cool for at least 10 minutes before serving.

Hot Mulled Cider

MAKES 6 CUPS (1.4 L)

Boiling water with aromatics to perfume your home is a common practice, but for the magically inclined, it's a spell. A simmer pot combines all four elements to cleanse energies and support an intention: water is the medium, warmed by stovetop fire and scented with the earth's gifts, all rising into the air as steam. Here, the ritual also simultaneously brews a potion that tastes of autumn. This mulled cider is simmered with warming, protective spices and cleansing citrus, all garnished with the apple's naturally occurring pentagram. Slice an apple from core to stem and you'll see the magical five-pointed star formed from the seeds, bobbing around in the cider like a magical talisman. Pair with a wedge of clothbound cheddar or Pecorino Plum Crumble (page 209).

6 cups (1.4 l) unfiltered apple cider

5 star anise pods

2 cinnamon sticks

2 teaspoons allspice

1 teaspoon whole cloves

½ lemon, thinly sliced into half-moons

½ orange, thinly sliced into half-moons

½ apple, thinly sliced into rounds

½ cup (120 ml) dark rum or rye whiskey (optional)

Set a medium pot on the stove and heat over medium-low.

Add the cider, star anise, cinnamon, allspice, cloves, and sliced lemon, orange, and apple. Stir three times counterclockwise, visualizing dark, stagnant energy evaporating into the air. Then stir three times clockwise, asking the powers of protection to flow into the pot.

Bring to a simmer and let cook for about 30 minutes. Stir in the rum or whiskey (if using), and serve hot.

Note: I like to keep the spices and fruit in there as garnishes, but you can strain them out as well.

Perfect Martini

MAKES 1 COCKTAIL

In my opinion, a cold martini is the most elegant and perfect of all cocktails. Just the literal spirit of the grain, rinsed with vermouth over ice, poured into a cold, clear glass, and garnished simply. The exact recipe depends on your preference, whether you favor gin's herbal bouquet or crisp and neutral vodka, stirred and strong or gently diluted with a shake, a twist of fragrant lemon, or a salty blue cheese–stuffed olive. I personally like my martini clean, never dirty, with a three-to-one ratio of gin to vermouth and a Spanish Gordal olive stuffed with Roquefort. Pair with a sheep's milk cheese, like Pecorino, Manchego, or a wedge of Roquefort.

FOR THE BLUE CHEESE OLIVES (makes 8)

1 ounce (28 g) creamy blue cheese, such as Roquefort or Bleu d'Auvergne

8 pitted green olives

FOR THE MARTINI

3 ounces (90 ml) gin or vodka

1 ounce (30 ml) dry white vermouth, preferably Cocchi or Dolin

Make the blue cheese olives: Cut the blue cheese into 8 even pieces. Stick the pieces inside the olives. Store in an airtight container in the fridge for up to 1 week.

Make the cocktail: Fill a cocktail glass with ice and set aside.

Fill a cocktail shaker with ice. Add the gin or vodka and the vermouth. Shake or stir for 30 seconds.

Dump the ice out of the glass, then strain the cocktail into it.

Garnish with a blue cheese olive.

Note: If you like a stiffer drink, use a four-to-one ratio. Stir instead of shake.

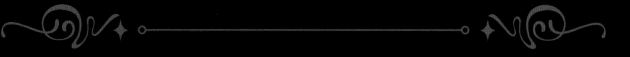

Zhongqiu Jie, the Mid-Autumn Moon Festival

The second most important festival in China, Zhongqiu Jie, falls on the full moon closest to the fall equinox. As far back as 3,000 years, ancient people would gather to worship the moon goddess Chang'e, offering prayers and sacrifices in the hopes that she'll return and bless next year's harvest. Nowadays, families celebrate by reuniting over dinners, making paper lanterns, eating moon cakes, and simply admiring the full lunation.

1 Harbison

is a spruce-wrapped, downy rind cheese from Jasper Hill Farm in Vermont. Each wheel is bound in bark harvested from trees on the same land as the farm. Look for a wheel nearing her expiration date and serve whole, with her top rind gently removed. She'll reward you with a custardy, dippable interior that tastes of evergreens, mushrooms, bacon, and mustard. Spread onto rye toast and top with a pickled shallot and slice of apple.

2 Red Rock

comes from fourth-generation cheesemaker Chris Roelli of Roelli Cheese Haus in Wisconsin. It is fluorescent orange with a bloomy, Brie-like rind and thick stripes of indigo molds. She has the classic tangy flavors of a cheddar, with notes of cave and forest floor near the rustic rind. Counter her salty streaks with a dollop of apple butter and Bourbon-Glazed Pecans.

3 Bandaged Cheddar

is shaped like a drum and bound in cloth, which creates a protective barrier around the cheese while allowing the rind to inhale her ambience as she ages. It's a laborious ritual, but results in a dry, buttery texture that crumbles like a scone, with deeply complex flavors ranging from soil and grass to juicy pineapple. I recommend Montgomery's Clothbound Cheddar from England, Flory's Truckle from Missouri, or Cabot Clothbound Cheddar from Vermont. Chip off a crumble and pair with salami and mustard.

MUSTARD

complements the acidic tang of the clothbound cheddar while offsetting the unctuous flavor.

SAUCISSON SEC

is a classic French salami that's flavored with black pepper and garlic.

TOASTED RYE BREAD

acts as a robustly flavored vehicle for the cheeses, perfuming the plate with licorice notes from the caraway seeds.

THYME

scents the plate with woodsy, autumnal aromas.

APPLE BUTTER

is cooked until caramelized and flavored with baking spices.

BOURBON-GLAZED PECANS

(page 213) bring a sweet, bourbon-spiked crunch that plays well off the salty cheeses.

2

3

APPLE SLICES

provide a crisp, palate-cleansing break from all the richness. To keep them from browning, soak them briefly in a one-to-four solution of lemon juice and water.

PICKLED SHALLOTS

(page 210) cut through the mouth-coating fats, teasing out the earthy flavors in the cheeses.

THE MABON CIDER PLATE

The apple harvest peaks during the equinox, making the speculated object of original sin the unofficial crop of Mabon. This platter honors the magical fruit in all her forms: sliced, cooked down into spreadable butter, and fermented into cider. While apples pair with nearly any cheese, none complement their crisp bite like cheddar, so I've featured two different styles. Pudding-soft Harbison brings a creamy element, Bourbon-Glazed Pecans add sweetness, while mustard, shallots, and rye toasts bring savory balance to this apple altar. I highly recommend imbibing hard cider: cheese loves its acidity, gentle sweetness, and playful effervescence, which makes it a natural pairing. Hard cider varies from dry to briny to sickly sweet. I recommend avoiding the latter, but feel free to experiment. For a nonalcoholic option, try fresh-pressed cider, straight out of the apple, or brew up some Hot Mulled Cider (page 215).

studded with dried fruits
and nuts provide a crunchy
vehicle for the cheese while
honoring the hard work of
harvest preservation.

THE

HARVEST MOON PLATE

The full lunation occurring closest to the
equinox is known as the harvest moon,
rising just after sunset. She appears full
for several days, illuminating the fields
so farmers can spend extra time
gathering their summer crops. Mabon
and her corresponding full moon mark
the end of harvest, the final push
before darkness swallows daylight
and we retreat back into our homes for
winter hibernation. Honor the harvest
moon by building an altar featuring a
small washed rind cheese, luminous
and surrounded by autumnal accompaniments. Pair with a medium-bodied
red wine or mug of Hot Mulled Cider
(page 215).

SAGE

is often used
in full moon
cleansing rituals.

FALL HONEY

is robust with notes
of maple, resin, and
molasses, flavors that
stand up well to the
cheese's funk.

1

ROASTED GRAPES

(page 213) represent the harvest and contrast the cheese's savory funk with rich sweetness.

PEARS

pair well with the custardy cheese and symbolize abundance, prosperity, and love.

1 Willoughby

is a petite wheel originally created by Marisa Mauro, founder of the cult-favorite butter company Ploughgate Creamery. When her creamery tragically burned down, she sold the recipe to Jasper Hill Farm, another Vermont cheesemaker that has since resurrected this gem of a cheese. The rosy rind is thin and tender, barely containing the plush custardy insides. She tastes of alliums, beef broth, roasting peanuts, and an unmistakable animal funk. If you can't find Willoughby, sub French Langres, Italian Capriolina, or Red Hawk from Cowgirl Creamery in California.

BRESAOLA

is an air-dried, salted beef with a deep purple hue and sweet notes of juniper and pepper.

MOON CAKES

are Chinese pastries filled with lotus-seed paste and traditionally eaten under the harvest moon during the mid-autumn festival.

1 Chèvre

serves as an excellent cheesy substitute for toasted marshmallows. Simply bring 4 ounces (115 g) of goat cheese to room temperature, and beat with a whisk until smooth and fluffy. Whisk in 2 teaspoons of maple syrup and transfer to a mini cast-iron skillet or other heatproof dish. Sprinkle with a teaspoon or two of sugar, making sure to fully coat the top, and use a brûlée torch to sear until the top bubbles and crisps. Pair with dark chocolate and graham crackers for an updated take on s'mores.

2 Brunost

is a Norwegian brown cheese that tastes like butterscotch and sticks to the roof of your mouth like peanut butter. Also known as gjetost, brunost is made by boiling the whey left over from cheesemaking until the liquid evaporates and the sugars caramelize. The resulting cheese is shaped into blocks and served in thin shavings, often on toast or waffles. You can find a wide variety of brunost in Scandinavian countries, but the brand Ski Queen (featured) is pretty easy to find elsewhere. Try a slice with roasted peanuts—it tastes just like brittle.

3 Smokey Blue

from Rogue Creamery in Oregon is cold-smoked over hazelnut shells, infusing her with subtle notes of bacon, vanilla custard, and autumnal leaf burnings. Though I often find that smoking overpowers a cheese's flavor, blues have enough but pungent blue molds can stand up to the smolder. If you can't find this one, swap any another smoked blue like Moody Blue from Roth Cheese. Pair with maple candies or dark chocolate.

GRAHAM CRACKERS
complement the sweet toasty flavors of the brunost and the brûléed chèvre.

ROASTED PEANUTS
bring salty, earthy flavors to contrast with the sweetness of the other pairings.

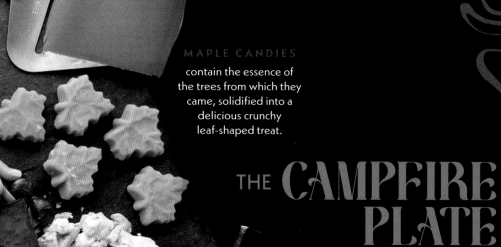

MAPLE CANDIES

contain the essence of the trees from which they came, solidified into a delicious crunchy leaf-shaped treat.

THE CAMPFIRE PLATE

3

This woodsy platter conjures memories of marshmallows toasting on an open fire, maple syrup on pancakes, and crisp autumn air perfumed with piles of dead leaves smoldering in the distance. It's an altar to the magic of the forest, as sweet as nostalgia itself. Serve surrounded with a collection of leaves, or better yet, bring the plate into the woods. Enjoy among the trees, aflame with the colors of fall, and thank them for their shelter and beauty. Pair with whiskey on the rocks, a dark stout, or even hot chocolate.

DARK CHOCOLATE

teases out the earthy notes in the blue cheese and couples with the brûléed goat cheese as a s'mores.

ROSEMARY

perfumes the platter with the aromatics of an enchanted forest.

SAMHAIN

Derived from the Irish word for "summer's end," Samhain marks the third and final harvest and the Celtic New Year. The fields are barren, the trees naked, and the air laced with the cold bite of the approaching winter. The veil between the worlds of the living and dead is at its thinnest, and spirits roam freely among us. It's the season of the witch: high time for divination, performing magical rituals, and leaving offerings for the dead. Embrace the darkness, for without shadow there is no light. Reflect on what you have planted, grown, and harvested throughout the cycle of the year before the wheel turns again, the light is reborn, and the cycle begins anew.

April 30 to May 1
✦ Southern Hemisphere ✦

Buckwheat Crepes

2 cups (480 ml) whole milk

3 large eggs

½ teaspoon kosher salt

⅔ cup buckwheat flour

⅓ cup all-purpose flour

2 tablespoons melted unsalted butter, plus an extra pat for cooking the crêpes

MAKES 6 TO 8 8-INCH [20-CM] CRÊPES

Buckwheat Crêpes with Mimolette and Onion Fig Jam

SERVES 6

Crêpes date back to the thirteenth century in the Brittany region of France, where they were first created to utilize leftover buckwheat porridge. Associated with Jupiter, buckwheat is an herb of abundance and wealth, though ironically it was a staple in the diets of peasants after arriving from its native homelands throughout Asia. Buckwheat is also used to cast a circle on the floor for creating a protective space in which to perform magical rituals. That's sort of what we're doing here: pouring a circle of buckwheat batter in a hot pan and enchanting the crêpe with caramelized onions, fig jam, salty ham, pumpkin-orange Mimolette, and an egg. Pair with coffee or a bright French red wine like pinot noir. Special thanks to my partner for helping me create this recipe!

3 tablespoons caramelized onions

⅓ cup (80 ml) fig jam

6 buckwheat crêpes

6 large eggs

Kosher salt

12 ounces (340 g) young Mimolette, at room temperature, freshly shredded

6 slices ham, such as French-style, Ibérico, or prosciutto

Freshly ground black pepper

Pinch of flaky salt

Make the crêpes: Add the milk, eggs, and salt to a blender and pulse until combined. Add both flours, and blend on high for 1 minute. Scrape into a large mixing bowl, cover, and chill for at least 2 hours, but preferably overnight.

Bring the batter to room temperature.

Heat a crêpe pan or a large nonstick skillet over medium. Add a pat of butter, using a pastry brush or paper towel to coat the pan. Ladle in about 3 tablespoons of batter. Swirl around the pan until it's evenly distributed.

Cook for about a minute, until the crêpe is set and you can easily loosen the edges with a spatula. Manifest a little confidence and flip the crêpe. Cook for another 30 seconds, then transfer to a wire rack to cool.

(continued on page 228)

BUCKWHEAT CRÊPES WITH MIMOLETTE
AND ONION FIG JAM, *continued*

Coat the pan again with the brush or towel, and add another pat if it looks dry. Ladle in more batter, and repeat the process until you use it all up.

Fill the crêpes: Roughly chop the onions and transfer to a small bowl. Stir in the jam and set aside.

Heat a skillet over medium. Place a crêpe in the center of the pan. Spread about a tablespoon of the onion and jam mixture over the center, leaving a 2-inch (5-cm) border.

Crack 1 egg into a small bowl, and gently slide it into the center of the crêpe. Use a spatula to spread the white evenly around, being careful not to leave the perimeter of the jam. Season with a pinch of kosher salt, and cover. Let cook until the white is set, about 3 minutes.

Uncover and sprinkle a handful of cheese around the yolk. Tear 1 slice of ham into strips, and layer on top of the cheese.

Carefully fold the edges of the crêpe toward the center like an envelope. Use a spatula to slide the crêpe onto a plate. Finish with black pepper and flaky salt to taste.

Note

Make sure to find a young Mimolette no more than 3 months old, which melts easily, unlike more mature wedges that are better for grating. If you can't find one, you can substitute a young Gouda, Edam, or even Red Rock, a cheddar-blue hybrid from Roelli Cheese Haus in Wisconsin.

Goddesses of the Darkness

Throughout the various mythologies, goddesses come in three main forms: maiden, mother, and crone. This illustrates the changing seasons: the fertility of spring, the life-giving harvest, and the death of winter. Since Samhain represents the transition from mother to crone, it's a prime time to work with fearsome and powerful death deities.

HEKATE, MOTHER OF WITCHES

Records of this moon goddess date back to ancient Greece, though evidence suggests that she's much older. She's the Queen of the Crossroads and closely associated with many animals, especially dogs and snakes. Leave her offerings of garlic, sweets, and wine, especially at a fork in the road.

MICTECACIHUATL, LADY OF THE DEAD

Some believe that this Aztec goddess is the origin of Santa Muerte. She is the guardian of the deceased and their remains, ruling over the underworld with her male counterpart, Mictlantecuhtli. She's often depicted as a skeleton, her jaw wide open to swallow the stars during the daytime.

KALI, THE DIVINE MOTHER

This fearsome Hindu goddess rules transformation and time. She's closely associated with both sexuality and violence, and even has her own day, Kali Puja, held around Halloween. She's said to live in cemeteries and is often depicted wearing a gilded crown and a necklace of skulls, her many arms clutching various weapons and a severed head.

BABA YAGA, THE SLAVIC CRONE

The original wicked witch is known for guiding souls to the afterlife, and cannibalizing children in fairy tales. She 's an earth goddess who resides in a woodland home balanced atop chicken legs and travels through the forest in a mortar and pestle.

Cheese-Stuffed Pumpkin

SERVES 2 TO 4

Stuffed with sweet, nutty Comte, cream, broth, and a little toasted bread, the sultry squash is roasted until the flesh caramelizes and the brew within bubbles with hot, cheesy decadence. I recommend using a sugar pumpkin, but you can also use acorn or red kuri squash. Just make sure to slice a little bit off the bottom so it sits flat. Pair with a dark, malty ale or Pomegranate Tonic (page 246).

2 slices sourdough, 1 inch (2.5 cm) thick

1½-pound (225 g) pumpkin or similar squash

1½ teaspoons neutral oil

Salt and freshly ground black pepper

½ cup (120 ml) vegetable or chicken broth

¼ cup (60 ml) heavy whipping cream

2 garlic cloves, minced

1 teaspoon chopped fresh sage

¼ teaspoon nutmeg

6 ounces (170 g) Comté or other Alpine-style cheese, at room temperature, freshly shredded

Preheat the oven to 450°F (230°C). Line a baking sheet with aluminum foil or a silicone mat.

Cut or tear the sourdough into cubes. Lightly toast them on the baking sheet until golden. Let cool completely. Set aside.

Slice the top off the pumpkin and scoop out all the strings and seeds. Place the pumpkin on the baking sheet and rub with the oil. Coat the inside, outside, and top lid. Sprinkle the inner cavity with a pinch each of salt and pepper.

In a liquid measuring cup, whisk together the broth, cream, garlic, sage, and nutmeg.

Place a third of the bread cubes inside the pumpkin. Pour a third of the broth mixture on top, then add a handful of cheese. Repeat until you reach the top. Finish with the rest of the cheese and a little black pepper.

Place the top lid next to the pumpkin to roast alongside. Bake until fork-tender, about 40 to 45 minutes. Let cool for 5 minutes.

Transfer the pumpkin to a serving platter and put the top back on for presentation. Scoop the fondue onto plates, making sure to get some of the cheese mixture and some of the soft pumpkin flesh too.

Prehistoric Pumpkins

The oldest record of pumpkins, which are native to the Americas, was found in an Oaxacan cave dating back at least 10,000 years, making squash one of the first cultivated foods. Ancient peoples roasted the flesh over the fire or even pounded and dried it into a jerky-like food.

Harvest Dressing

- 2 tablespoons cider vinegar
- 2 tablespoons onion jam
- 1 tablespoon whole-grain mustard
- 1 garlic clove, grated or minced
- ½ teaspoon freshly ground black pepper
- ¼ teaspoon black salt
- ¼ cup extra-virgin olive oil

MAKES ⅓ CUP (79 ML)

Harvest Salad with Brie Toasts

SERVES 4

Kale is a hearty crop that's easy to grow and ready to harvest by the end of October, so it makes sense why it was so popular for Samhain customs. Here it's tossed in a sweet oniony vinaigrette, with roasted squash, sprinkled with pomegranate seeds and pepitas, then served alongside toasts topped with melted Brie. It's a celebration of the final harvest that honors the cruciferous vegetable's roots in Halloween tradition. Serve alongside a hot cup of Witches' Brew (page 247) or a bold red wine.

1 pound (455 g) delicata squash

1 tablespoon canola or other neutral oil

2 teaspoons Magic Salt (page 243)

1 teaspoon chopped fresh sage

2 bunches lacinato kale, washed and dried

4 slices sourdough, 1 inch thick

8 ounces (255 g) Brie, thinly sliced

Diamond Crystal kosher salt

Freshly ground black pepper

¼ cup (45 g) pomegranate seeds

3 tablespoons roasted and salted pepitas

⅓ cup Harvest Dressing (opposite page)

Make the dressing: In a medium mixing bowl, whisk together the vinegar, onion jam, mustard, garlic, black pepper, and black salt. Slowly drizzle in the olive oil, whisking continuously until smooth and creamy.

Make the salad: Preheat the oven to 475°F (245°C). Line a baking sheet with parchment paper or a silicone baking mat.

Peel the skin off the squash. Cut the squash in half, then scoop the guts out of the cavity. Cut the squash into ½-inch (1.3-cm) slices.

Transfer the squash to a large mixing bowl, and drizzle with the oil. Toss to coat, then season with the Magic Salt and sage. Toss again, then spread out onto the prepared baking sheet.

Bake until browned and fork-tender, about 25 to 30 minutes. Let cool completely.

Remove the stems from the kale, and discard. Slice the leaves thinly, and transfer to a large salad bowl.

(continued on page 234)

Samhain's Superfood

Celtic peoples have used kale in their Samhain celebrations since at least the Middle Ages, when the leafy greens made their way to the British Isles. One of the most popular rituals was called "pulling the stalks." Eligible singles would don blindfolds and sneak onto the fields on Halloween night to pluck kale from the earth. They'd read the stalks—using factors like length, density, and patterns in the dirt caked onto the leaves—to divine clues about their future spouse.

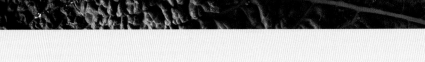

HARVEST SALAD WITH BRIE TOASTS, *continued*

Drizzle the kale with half of the dressing and toss to coat, massaging the leaves with your hands. Let rest for 10 minutes.

Meanwhile, toast the sourdough until golden brown. Layer the Brie on top of the toasts. Sprinkle with a pinch of pepper. Broil for 1 minute, until the cheese is browned and bubbly.

Add the squash to the kale and toss to coat. Taste a leaf for seasoning, and add salt and pepper as needed. Transfer to salad plates, then drizzle with the rest of the dressing. Sprinkle with the pomegranate seeds and pepitas, then serve with the toasts.

How to Build an Offering Platter

Begin by deciding who you want to make the offering to: an ancestor, deity, or even a planetary body. Remember that we're all made up of the same organic matter. Your ancestors are everywhere, from your literal relatives to the moon above. See the Offering Plate on page 252 for an example.

Make the plate personal by adding a family recipe or foods important to your chosen deity. Gather photos or tokens from your loved ones.

After building your plate, **say a prayer of gratitude** for all the blessings and for those who came before you. Set an additional plate out for your ancestors and serve them each a portion. You can even set out glasses and pour their favorite libation.

As you eat, catch them up on your life and **ask for what you need.** Alternatively, you can host a "dumb supper," which is when you eat in silence. After you finish your meal, leave their plate out overnight, preferably on an ancestor altar.

The next morning, bring the plate to a natural area to **give the food back to the land,** or compost it. Make sure you don't leave anything out that could make an animal sick, like chocolate or alliums.

Turnip Tartiflette

SERVES 2 TO 4

Carving a turnip is very difficult (trust me, I've tried), but you can still pay homage with this Turnip Tartiflette. This classic French dish is usually made with potatoes, but turnips add a nutty flavor, velvety texture, and protective energies. Reblochon is the traditional cheese for tartiflette, but she's very difficult to source, so I recommend any pudgy washed rind, such as Taleggio, Oma from von Trapp Farmstead in Vermont, or even shredded raclette. Pair with lightly dressed greens and a glass of bold red wine, malty beer, or Pomegranate Tonic (page 246).

1 pound (455 g) turnips

¼ pound (115 g) bacon, cut into 1-inch (2.5-cm) pieces

1 leek, thoroughly cleaned and thinly sliced

2 teaspoons chopped fresh thyme, plus more for garnish

2 cloves garlic, minced or grated

¾ cup (180 ml) dry white wine

¼ cup (60 ml) heavy whipping cream

¼ teaspoon nutmeg

½ teaspoon kosher salt

2 teaspoons Magic Salt (page 243)

8 ounces (225 g) washed rind cheese, thinly sliced

Preheat the oven to 350°F (175°C).

Peel the turnips, then slice thinly. (A mandolin makes an easy job of this.)

Line a plate with paper towels and set aside.

Heat a large ovenproof skillet over medium and add the bacon. Cook until browned and crisped. Transfer the bacon to the paper towel–lined plate and dab to remove excess fat. Drain the fat from the pan, reserving 1 tablespoon.

Cook the leeks and thyme in the reserved fat over medium heat until golden and sweetly fragrant, about 5 minutes. Add the garlic and cook until fragrant, about 1 minute.

In a liquid measuring cup, whisk together the wine, cream, and nutmeg. Add the mixture to the skillet, then bring to a simmer. Stir with a wooden spoon to scrape up any browned bits. Add the turnips and sprinkle with the kosher salt and Magic Salt. Stir and simmer until the liquid reduces by half and the turnips are fork-tender, about 25 minutes.

Turn off the heat and add the bacon back into the skillet. Stir to distribute, then evenly layer the cheese on top.

Bake for about 20 minutes, until brown and bubbling. Remove from the oven and let cool for about 5 minutes. Garnish with a sprig of thyme and serve straight out of the skillet.

Store leftovers in an airtight container in the fridge for 3 to 5 days.

Stingy Jack

Carving jack-o'-lanterns for Halloween is a centuries-old tradition, but the originals were made of turnips rather than pumpkins. This ritual comes from the old Irish folktale of Stingy Jack, a man so evil that neither heaven nor hell would accept him. With nowhere to go, Jack was doomed to an eternity spent roaming the darkness with nothing but a piece of coal inside a turnip to light his way. To ward off evil spirits such as Jack of the Lantern, people would carve turnips with ghoulish faces and insert a glowing ember inside. When Irish immigrants brought their Samhain traditions to the New World, they swapped the root vegetables for pumpkins.

This recipe is perfect, thanks to my mother, who is far more meticulous than I and loves immersing herself in tweaking a recipe until she renders it foolproof. Her willpower and talent created the framework for several recipes in this book, from the Corn Spoonbread (page 172) to the Lemon Pizza (page 178), where I just added a little cheese and published it.

I highly recommend putting in the extra effort and making her pie dough recipe and brewing your own applesauce, but as Ina Garten says, store-bought is just fine.

Gouda Apple Galette

MAKES 1 GALETTE

I'll be the first to admit that I'm not a great baker—it's too precise, too repetitive, too finicky a practice. I don't want to labor for hours only to pull a burnt yet still somehow underdone pie out of the oven. That's why I love the rustic simplicity of the free-form pie known as the galette. Get yourself a wedge of well-aged Gouda. You want a warm amber hue and lots of crunchy cheese crystals, which are amino acid clusters that form when the curd's web of fat and protein breaks down and leaves behind constellations of toothsome crystalline tyrosine. Serve with a malty brown ale or Hot Mulled Cider (page 215).

FOR THE PIE DOUGH

1⅓ cups (160 g) all-purpose flour, plus more for rolling out the galette

1½ teaspoons granulated sugar

¾ teaspoon Diamond Crystal kosher salt

¾ cup (170 g) unsalted butter, chilled

FOR THE APPLESAUCE
(makes about 1 cup / 240 ml)

1½ pounds (685 g) sweet apples, such as Gala or Golden Delicious

1 tablespoon light brown sugar

½ teaspoon cinnamon

½ teaspoon freshly grated ginger

2 teaspoons lemon zest (about half a lemon)

1 tablespoon lemon juice (about half a lemon)

FOR THE GALETTE

1 pie dough

1 pound (455 g) baking apples, such as Granny Smith or Braeburn

1 tablespoon light brown sugar

½ teaspoon cinnamon

¼ teaspoon cardamom

¼ teaspoon kosher salt

2 teaspoons lemon juice (about half a lemon)

½ cup (120 ml) applesauce

1 tablespoon unsalted butter, chopped

1 teaspoon chopped fresh thyme

1 large egg, lightly beaten

2 ounces (55 g) aged Gouda

½ teaspoon granulated sugar

Vanilla ice cream, to serve

(continued on page 240)

Make the pie dough: In a medium mixing bowl, whisk together the flour, sugar, and salt.

Cut the butter into 6 rectangular pieces. Add to the dry ingredients and toss to coat.

Dump the mixture onto your clean work surface. Using a rolling pin, work the butter into the flour until it forms long flexible strips. Use a bench scraper as needed to scrape the butter off your rolling pin and work surface.

Gather the mixture into a loose pile, then drizzle 4 tablespoons of ice water over it. Use your hands and a bench scraper to toss the mixture until the water is distributed.

Gather into a rectangular pile. Roll out the dough into a long rectangle with short ends about 8 inches (20 cm) wide, then use the bench scraper to fold the dough into thirds, like folding a letter. It will be very crumbly and loose, but don't panic.

Using the bench scraper to help, turn the rectangle 90 degrees and repeat rolling and folding, gathering loose bits of dough from the outer edges into the center and flouring the surface as needed. Repeat rolling and folding a third time. The dough should be somewhat homogenous and creamy-looking with some dry bits around the edges. Squeeze a bit in your palm; it should loosely hold together. If not, repeat rolling and folding.

Wrap the folded dough in plastic, then press it into a compact disk about 1 inch (2.5 cm) thick. Chill for at least 30 minutes, or up to

3 days if making ahead. You can freeze the dough for up to 3 months.

Make the applesauce: Peel, core, and roughly chop the apples. Transfer to a medium saucepan and heat over medium-low.

Add the brown sugar, cinnamon, ginger, salt, lemon zest, and 1 tablespoon of water. Stir to combine, cover, and bring to a simmer.

Let cook until soft, about 15 minutes. Mash the apples until they're smooth and pulpy.

Stir in the lemon juice. Let cool completely.

Make the galette: Preheat the oven to 400°F (200°C). Line a baking sheet with parchment paper or a silicone mat.

On a lightly floured surface, roll out the pie dough into a 12- to 14-inch (30- to 35-cm) round or oval about ⅛ inch (3 mm) thick. Don't worry if there are cracks around the perimeter. It's part of the rustic charm. Just make sure to dust the surface and rolling pin with flour as needed and rotate the dough often to prevent wider cracks. If the dough sticks to the surface, lift on one side and scatter flour underneath before continuing. Roll the dough onto your pin, then unfurl it onto the lined baking sheet.

Core and slice the apples. Set aside.

In a medium mixing bowl, stir together the brown sugar, cinnamon, cardamom, and salt. Whisk in the lemon juice. Add the apple slices and toss to coat.

GOUDA APPLE GALETTE, *continued*

Spoon the applesauce over the galette, leaving a 3-inch (8-cm) border.

Starting from the outer edge of the applesauce, layer the apples in a concentric circle that ends in the center. Dot with the butter and sprinkle with the thyme.

Fold the edges of the dough up and over the apples, pleating as needed and being careful that the folded edge of the dough doesn't tear (if it does, patch with scraps of dough and pinch to seal).

Brush the crust with the egg.

Use a microplane to grate the Gouda over the whole galette, including the crust. Finish with a sprinkle of granulated sugar.

Place the galette in the oven and immediately reduce the heat to 375°F (190°C). Bake, rotating halfway through, until the crust is deep golden brown everywhere, the apples are tender, and the juices are bubbling, about 45 minutes. Let the galette cool for 2 hours on parchment paper before serving.

Serve with vanilla ice cream and an extra grating of Gouda.

Apple Divination

Historically, apples have been popular tools for telling the future. Some would peel the fruit in one long piece, searching for shapes and letters when it dropped to the floor. Others would wet the seeds, each one representing a suitor, stick them to their cheek, and let them fall. The last seed remaining represented their one true love.

Wine jelly technique comes from an article by Kat Kinsman in Food & Wine *magazine.*

Mulled Wine Jelly

MAKES ABOUT 1 CUP (240 ML)

This spiked and spiced jelly celebrates transformation: grapes fermented into wine, mulled with spices, and finally solidified into jelly. Pair this mulled wine jelly with bold blues and aged sheep's milk cheeses or serve on the Offering Plate (page 252) to provide a sweet libation to deities or ancestors passing through the veil into the world of the living.

1 cup (240 ml) red wine, such as Merlot, Zinfandel, or Grenache

1 tablespoon brandy

1 orange slice

4 whole cloves

2 star anise pods

1 cinnamon stick

1 tablespoon powdered pectin

1 cup (200 g) granulated sugar

½ teaspoon citric acid

To a medium saucepan, add the wine, brandy, orange slice, cloves, anise, and cinnamon. Bring to a simmer, cover, and cook for 30 minutes. Remove the orange and spices, and discard.

Measure out the wine. If it has reduced, then add a little more to bring it back to 1 cup. Bring to a boil. Add the pectin and whisk constantly for 1 minute.

Stir in the sugar and boil until it dissolves and the wine thickens slightly, about 1 more minute. Remove from the heat, stir in the citric acid, and let sit for 15 minutes.

Skim off any foam, then transfer the wine mixture to a 10-ounce jar. Cool for 30 minutes, then cover and chill for 6 hours. Store for up to 2 weeks in the fridge.

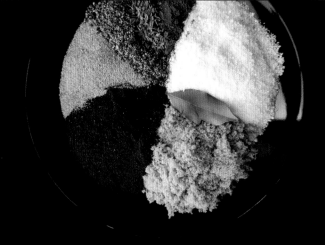

Magic Salt

MAKES ½ CUP (150 G)

Since it holds the power to ward off spoilage, salt has become a popular ingredient in protection and purification spells. Here, it's infused with brown sugar for attraction, paprika for passion, garlic and black pepper for protection, thyme and nutmeg for luck, cayenne and cinnamon to quicken your spell, and a bay leaf for prosperity. Use as a rub for meats, sprinkle over root vegetables before roasting, or use as a finishing salt over the Harvest Salad (page 233).

¼ cup (75 g) kosher salt

3 tablespoons light brown sugar

1½ tablespoons paprika

1 tablespoon freshly ground black pepper

1 tablespoon garlic powder

2 teaspoons dried thyme

1 teaspoon cayenne pepper

½ teaspoon nutmeg

¼ teaspoon cinnamon

1 bay leaf

Add all ingredients to a mason jar. Cover and shake to combine. Remove the lid and place the jar under the moonlight to charge. If you wish, you can speak an intention over the salt as it charges. In the morning, cover the jar and store it in a cool, dry place.

Note: You can also use this salt in magical workings. Rub a candle in a little olive oil then roll in the salt, or sprinkle a little in front of your doorway on the eve of Samhain to protect and bless your home in the year to come.

Note

Don't wash the mushrooms: they'll soak up too much moisture. Instead, use a pastry brush or clean towel to gently brush off any visible dirt.

Mushrooms are integral to decay and transformation. They help decompose plants and animals, generating nutrient-rich soils. Similarly, the tiny fungi that bloom on the rinds of cheeses like Brie break down fats and proteins, creating soft, unctuous textures.

Mushroom Pâté

MAKES 2 CUPS (110 G)

Mushrooms are magical. They seem to sprout almost out of thin air after a cleansing rainfall, flecking forest floors and adorning fallen trees. Naturally, they're heavily associated with death, rebirth, and transformation. Eat them to let go of anything you'd like to compost, unhealthy behavioral patterns, limiting beliefs, or even a toxic relationship. Not only do they play an essential role in the circle of life, they are also an extremely nutritious food source. Sautéed with butter, herbs, and a little ricotta for richness, they also make for an excellent vegetarian pâté. Pair with a fresh baguette and Brie to tease out the rinds' mushroomy notes or serve on the Grounding Plate (page 250) to reconnect with your roots and the element of earth.

1 pound (455 g) mushrooms, such as cremini, shiitake, blue oyster, or a mixture

2 tablespoons unsalted butter

1 shallot, minced

2 teaspoons chopped fresh sage

1 teaspoon fresh thyme

1 teaspoon kosher salt, divided

½ teaspoon freshly ground black pepper, divided

4 garlic cloves, grated

1½ tablespoons Dijon mustard

4 ounces (115 g) ricotta

Brush any dirt off the mushrooms. Roughly chop them and set aside.

Heat a large skillet over medium heat. Add the butter.

When it starts to foam, add the shallot, sage, thyme, ½ teaspoon salt, and ¼ teaspoon pepper. Cook, stirring occasionally, until the shallots are golden and fragrant, about 3 to 4 minutes.

Add the mushrooms and cook until they release their moisture and start to brown, about 15 minutes. Make sure to stir them every couple of minutes to prevent burning.

Add the garlic and cook for another 2 minutes, stirring constantly.

Remove from the heat and let cool.

Transfer to the bowl of a food processor and add the mustard, ricotta, and the remaining salt and pepper. Blend until smooth.

Store covered in the fridge for up to 1 week.

Pomegranate Tonic

MAKES 1 TONIC

Pomegranates are closely associated with death and the underworld, especially according to Greek mythology. They're known as the fruit of the dead and the blood of Adonis, the god of rebirth. After eating six pomegranate seeds, Persephone was doomed to spend all of fall and winter in Hades. This uplifting spritzer mixes their juice with that of the blood orange, which is similarly rich in antioxidants and vitamin C. Pair with the Offering Plate (page 252).

2 ounces (60 ml) pomegranate juice

1 ounce (30 ml) freshly squeezed blood orange juice

2 ounces (60 ml) tonic water

1 blood orange wheel, to garnish

Fill a 12-ounce (360-ml) rocks glass with a large ice cube. Mix the juices and pour over the ice. Top with the tonic water and garnish with a wheel of blood orange.

Witches' Brew

MAKES 1 POTION

This hot, calming brew is essentially a hot toddy spiked with an enchanted oxymel, conjured to protect you from the perils of cold and flu season. An oxymel is a medicinal concoction of vinegar and raw honey that dates back hundreds of years. It's often steeped with herbs and spices such as the case with Fire Cider. I love the ritual of creating the vinegar infusion, filling a jar with powerful ingredients, and patiently waiting as they steep in the vinegar, before straining them out and sweetening the brew with honey.

1 cup (240 ml) water

1 lemon slice

1 small sprig fresh rosemary

1 tablespoon Fire Cider
(page 257)

½ teaspoon freshly squeezed
lemon juice

Raw honey

Bourbon or rum (optional)

Bring the water to a boil, pour it into a mug, and top with the lemon slice and rosemary. Let cool for 3 minutes, until it's drinking temperature but still warm. Stir in the Fire Cider, lemon juice, honey to taste, and bourbon or rum if you're imbibing.

1 Barely Buzzed

from Beehive Cheese in Utah is sweet, crunchy, and cloaked in coffee grounds. She's similar to a cheddar, but with more tropical notes of pineapple due to the addition of a culture called *Lactobacillus helveticus.* Her best feature is the layer of lavender and coffee grounds on her rind, both of which are traditional offerings to the dead. If you can't find her, you can always substitute Espresso BellaVitano from Sartori or another sweet cheddar-style cheese without the caffeinated coating. Pair with a peanut butter cup or a dried fig.

2 Mimolette

is a French cheese with a dusty, moon-like rind. The cratered exterior is formed by an army of tiny, spider-like cheese mites that eat away at the surface molds, aerating the cheese as she ages. The best wheels mature for at least 9 months, which gives the cheese enough time to form crunchy crystals and toasty notes of butter-scotch followed by a slight tang reminiscent of Cheez-Its. Candy corn makes an unexpected yet perfect pairing: together they taste like honeycomb.

3 St Albans

from Vermont Creamery is a cow's milk cheese with a texture so soft that she's sold in a little crock to keep the wheels from falling apart. If you can't find St Albans, substitute the French cheeses she's based on: Saint-Félicien or Saint-Marcellin. Any of them are delectable when smeared onto a ghost-shaped cookie with a little pumpkin butter.

DRIED FIGS offer sweetness and look like little shrunken heads.

PUMPKIN SEEDS symbolize the abundance of the final harvest.

SPICED PUMPKIN BUTTER brings the deep, spicy flavors of the final harvest's most iconic crop.

CHOCOLATE PEANUT BUTTER CUPS are a sweet treat that complements the coffee-coated cheese.

1

2

CANDY CORN

is festive and
complements the flavors
of the Mimolette.

3

APPLES

are key to the harvest
bounty during
Samhain and pair
with all the cheeses.

GHOST COOKIES

represent the spirits that
roam the earth on
Halloween night.

THE SAMHAIN PLATE

Nearly all of our beloved Halloween traditions are rooted in Samhain customs. Trick-or-treating references the practice of setting out offerings to the spirits that are passing through. Jack-o'-lanterns are protection wards against demons. Haunted houses are a way of confronting our fear of the waxing darkness and the ghosts of our past. Samhain is the most famous spoke in the Wheel of the Year because it's so closely associated with witchcraft and all the darkest aspects of life that fascinate so many of us. It's also the Celtic New Year, a time for reflection and new beginnings. This platter honors Samhain's roots as well as modern-day Halloween celebrations with pumpkins, ghost-shaped cookies, and dried apples. Pair with mulled cider, stout, Pomegranate Tonic (page 246), or a mug of Witches' Brew (page 247) or a healthful year ahead.

WHOLE WHEAT CRACKERS

add an earthy sweet canvas for the pâté and cheeses.

MUSHROOM PÂTÉ

(page 244) brings umami-laden flavors of an enchanted forest.

THE

GROUNDING PLATE

As the veil between the realm of the living and that of the underworld thins, nature dies all around us. The leaves fall, making skeletons of the once-lush trees, and any fruits or vegetables left unharvested wither and rot back into the earth. It's a wonderful time to reflect on what you'd like to compost in your own life and reconnect with your roots. Grounding is an essential practice, especially with the chaos of the holiday season fast approaching. Find a quiet place, breathe deeply, and indulge in the ritual of this simple cheese plate filled with earthy ingredients like root vegetable chips, onion jam, and funky cheeses. Pair with a bold red wine, Pomegranate Tonic (page 246) or a hot mug of Witches's Brew (page 247).

1

ROOT VEGETABLE CHIPS

add subtle, starchy sweetness and the fiery hue of autumn leaves.

BEEF SALAMI

has a warm red hue and rich flavor that complements the earthy cheeses.

2

THYME

grounds the plate with healing, purifying powers.

HAZELNUTS

flirt with the nutty notes in the cheeses and offer protective energies.

ONION JAM

contrasts with the salty flavors and teases out the notes of allium in the Saint Nectaire.

1 Morbier PDO

is a washed rind cow's milk cheese from the Jura region of France with an azure line of ash bisecting her ivory paste. The ghostly layer isn't only striking but also serves a protective purpose. Back in the day, the farmers in this region would deliver their milk yields to the village cheesemaker, who would craft huge wheels of Comté. When the harsh mountain conditions impeded their journey, the farmers would make their own cheese. Their small herds didn't yield enough to make a whole wheel, so they'd culture the evening milk, ladle it into molds, then dust it with ash to ward off insects. In the morning, the farmers would pour the curds from the morning milk over the ash, preserving the shadowy line within. Pair with a slice of salami or onion jam and rye bread.

2 Saint-Nectaire

is a French washed rind that's prone to mishandling, due to her beautiful yet sensitive rind. When she's at her best, she tastes of soft, wet soil and mossy stumps, with notes of hazelnuts and fresh hay. The cows graze on volcanic-rich soil in the Auvergne region, feasting on wild thyme, licorice, cranberry, yarrow, and other mystical flora, which all contribute to the resulting flavor of the cheese. Pair with hazelnuts to complement the cheese's naturally nutty notes.

THE
OFFERING
PLATE

Samhain forces us to confront death, and not only that of the natural world. It's also time to remember those you've lost. One way to do this is by leaving out offerings on Halloween, a simple sacrifice that expresses gratitude to those who watch over you from the spirit realm. Not only does this keep your loved ones alive through remembrance, but it helps you manifest your desires in the year ahead, whether you want protection, guidance, or blessings on a new venture. Use the following as inspiration but make it personal to you and include things that your ancestors loved (see page 235 for more information on how to build an offering plate). Pair with a light-bodied red wine, champagne, or any libation with cultural significance to your lineage or ancestry.

MARIGOLDS

traditionally decorate altars on Día de los Muertos because they're thought to attract the souls of the dead.

BLOOD ORANGES

are beautiful and uplifting, perfect for wishing ancestors happiness in the afterlife.

1 Wabash Cannonball

from Capriole Goat Cheese in Indiana is an adorable 3-ounce goat cheese with a bone-white paste that contrasts against her ash-coated exterior. Her wrinkled, tomb-gray rind tastes of button mushrooms, while her dense, velvety interior is lemon-fresh. My dearly departed grandfather loved the goat cheeses I used to bring him, so I always make sure to include one on any ancestor offering plate. Pair with a dollop of mulled wine and a charcoal cracker.

DARK CHOCOLATE

contrasts with the salty cheese while also wishing those who've passed a sweet return to the world of the living.

PEPITAS

are used in protection spells, warding off evil spirits from entering your home.

MULLED WINE JELLY

(page 242) acts as a libation, which is defined as a ritual offering of a beverage to ancestors, spirits, and deities.

CHARCOAL CRACKERS

offer a crunchy bed for the soft goat cheese.

GLOSSARY

AFFINE: To age cheese. It means "refine" in French and refers to the art of curing a cheese in a carefully controlled environment to help develop all the sultry molds and bacteria that make a cheese taste so delicious.

AFFINEUR: A cheese nanny. This is someone who takes care of cheese wheels as they age and mature.

ALPINE-STYLE: A firm, rugged style of cheese from the Alps durable enough to last through long winters. Cheese experts nerd out over the incredible flavor complexity in Alpine cheeses. They're full of toasty, nutty notes and often taste like caramelized onions and beef stock. Examples include Gruyère, Comté, and Pleasant Ridge Reserve from Uplands Cheese.

AMMONIATED: A term that describes cheese that smells or tastes of ammonia. This is not a good thing. It means a cheese was mishandled or has over ripened. If your cheese smells like a litter box, don't eat it. It probably won't hurt you, but it won't taste great either.

ANNATTO: This is what cheese-makers add to cheddar and Mimolette to make it orange. It's an all-natural plant-based dye that's virtually tasteless and odorless, but it looks fierce.

ATHAME: A ritual knife often associated with the element of air or fire. It can be substituted with a kitchen or cheese knife.

BELTANE: The cross-quarter fertility festival that falls on May 1.

BLOOMY/SOFT-RIPENED: Cheeses that ripen from the outside in. They have thin, downy rinds with soft, oozy, or pudgy insides. Examples include Brie, Valençay, and robiola.

BLUE CHEESE: The funky cheeses with veins and pockets of blue mold, like Roquefort, Stilton, and Bayley Hazen Blue. Some also have blue molds on the outer rind.

CASEIN: The main protein in milk. This is what makes milk coagulate and also what makes cheese so stretchy.

CAULDRON: A common magical instrument also used for practical purposes like cooking and washing. It is associated with goddess energy, the womb, and the element of water.

CAVE OR CELLAR: This is where a lot of cheeses are aged. A cheese cave or cellar has the optimum airflow, temperature, and humidity levels to keep cheeses consistently comfortable as they mature.

CHALICE: A ritual cup associated with the element of water. It can be substituted with any glass or cup, especially if it's a particularly favored one.

CHEDDARING: The process for making cheddar. After the cheese is coagulated, the curds are drained, cut into smaller pieces, and pressed into big slabs, which are stacked on top of each other. Then these slabs are turned. This drains the whey and helps develop that tangy acidity in cheddar. The slabs are then cut up again and molded for aging.

CHEESE CRYSTAL: This is what I call the crunchy bits inside aged Goudas and Parmigiano. It's actually clusters of an amino acid called tyrosine that form as cheese ages.

CHEESEMONGER: The knowledgeable cheese lovers who care for cheese at the counter and help you find the right cheese.

CHÈVRE: The French term for a cheese made from goat's milk.

CLOTHBOUND CHEDDAR: A drum of cheddar that's wrapped in a muslin bandage, as opposed to classic block cheddar.

COAGULATE: See "curdle."

COOKED CHEESE: Some hard cheeses are made by heating, or "cooking," the curd to help release extra moisture. This preps cheeses like Alpine styles for long periods of aging.

CORN DOLLY: A figurine made of woven corn or grain husks to represent the harvest goddess.

COVEN: A group of witches who gather together for magical workings.

CREAMLINE: The soft layer of ooze right between the rind and paste. It's one of the most sensual parts of bloomy-rinded cheeses like Brie and Camembert.

CRONE: The final aspect of the triple goddess that takes the form of an old woman. She is symbolized by the waning moon.

CURDLE: When rennet is added to milk, it separates, or "curdles," into solids and liquid. Also called "coagulate."

DIVINATION: The act of searching for knowledge, often about the future. Forms include tarot, scrying, tea leaves, and tyromancy.

EVOCATION: The act of inviting an energy or deity to join you in a sacred space.

EYES: The little dots and holes in cheese. Think of a classic Swiss Emmentaler.

FAE/FAIRY: Mythical creatures that love mischief and are said to be most active during Beltane and midsummer.

FAMILIAR: A nonhuman assistant to a witch, such as a cat or dog.

FARMSTEAD CHEESE: A cheese that is made using milk from animals that live on the same premises as the creamery.

FORMAGGIO: Italian for "cheese."

FRESH CHEESE: A category of unaged cheeses. These high-moisture cheeses with no rinds are super refreshing and amazing in the summertime. Think burrata, feta, and cheese curds.

FROMAGE: French for "cheese."

GOUDA: A tasty firm cheese with a rounded rind, originally from the Netherlands. She's meltable and tangy when young and becomes crunchy and butterscotch-sweet when she's aged.

GRIMOIRE: A magical book of rituals and spells.

HALLOWEEN: All Hallows' Eve, or the holiday that falls on the eve of Samhain (October 31).

IMBOLC: The cross-quarter festival that falls on February 1 and celebrates the first stirrings of spring.

INVOCATION: The act of inviting an energy or deity into your physical self.

LIBATION: A beverage offered to spirits, ancestors, or deities.

LITHA: The festival that celebrates the summer solstice and the peak of summer.

LUGHNASADH: The cross-quarter festival that falls on August 1 and celebrates the grain harvest.

MABON: The festival celebrating the autumn equinox and the harvest.

MAGIC: The act of creating change through supernatural forces.

MAIDEN: The first aspect of the triple goddess represented by springtime and the waxing moon.

MAYPOLE: A pole that's covered in interwoven ribbons to celebrate spring and symbolize the union of the god and goddess. It's erected on Beltane or Litha.

MOLDS: These are partly responsible for turning rinds into rich ecosystems, which result in some crazy tasty cheeses. There are a lot of yeasts and bacteria that help with that too.

MOTHER: The second aspect of the triple goddess symbolized by the harvest and the full moon.

OCCULT: A category of supernatural beliefs. The literal definition is "hidden" or "secret."

OSTARA: The festival celebrating the spring equinox and nature's rebirth.

PAGAN: A term for anyone who practices an earth-based religion.

PASTE: The inside layer beneath the rind. It's basically the "meat" of a cheese.

PASTEURIZATION: The process of heating up milk to kill bacteria.

PDO/AOC/DOP: "Protected Denomination of Origin," in various languages. These labels are a sign that the government is regulating where and how the cheese is made to ensure that she's true to her name.

PENTACLE: A five-pointed star inside a circle.

PENTAGRAM: A five-pointed star that represents the four elements and spirit. It has become the symbol of Wicca.

QUESO: Spanish for "cheese."

RAW MILK: Untreated milk that hasn't been pasteurized. This milk has all kinds of enzymes and bacteria that bring out various unique tastes and textures when they become cheese.

RIND: The protective outer layer that's basically the cheese's skin. Some are soft, some are stinky, some are edible, and some are coated in wax or cloth.

RITUAL: A systematic demonstration with a magical purpose.

RUMINANT: An even-toed, herbivorous animal with a four-compartment stomach. This classification includes all dairy animals, like goats, sheep, and cows.

RUNES: The Teutonic alphabet often inscribed onto small tiles. Modern pagans use it for divination or for writing spells.

SABBAT: One of the eight festivals featured in the Wheel of the Year.

SAMHAIN: The cross-quarter festival that falls on November 1 and marks the end of harvest season.

SCRYING: A form of divination involving gazing upon a black mirror, a lit candle, or incense smoke.

SIGIL: A symbol with magical power. The name comes from the Latin *sigillum*, meaning "sign."

SPELL: A magical ritual with the intention to attract, banish, or cause change in another form.

SYMPATHETIC MAGIC: A ritual that uses correspondence or symbolism to achieve an effect. Example: lighting a Yule log aflame to lure the sun back.

TAROT: A set of divinatory cards containing pictures or symbols.

TERROIR: The environment in which something is made, which can create unique flavors in a cheese. This is why French Comté tastes so different from Swiss Gruyère, even though they are made with a similar technique.

TRIPLE GODDESS: All three aspects of the goddess: maiden, mother, and crone.

WAND: A staff associated with the element of fire or air. It can be substituted with a spoon, preferably wooden.

WARD: A ritual with the intention of banishing or protecting.

WASHED RIND: A cheese that is washed in a brine or solution to help certain bacteria grow. Most of these guys are quite stanky and often taste like beef and mustard. Examples include Taleggio or Grayson from Meadow Creek Dairy.

WHEEL OF THE YEAR: The eight sabbats that evoke the eternal ever-turning cycle of time.

WHEY: The leftover liquid from cheesemaking. Sometimes people create some fire cheeses out of it, like ricotta and gjetost.

WICCA: A Western nature-based religion originating in the early twentieth century.

WITCH: A practitioner of magic.

YULE: The festival celebrating the winter solstice and the rebirth of the sun.

Fire Cider

- 1 ½ ounce (45 g) ginger, grated
- ½ ounce turmeric, sliced
- ½ ounce (15 g) fresh horseradish, peeled and grated
- 1 small onion, peeled and sliced
- 3 garlic cloves, peeled and smashed
- 2 star anise pods
- 1 cinnamon stick
- 1 teaspoon black peppercorns
- 1 teaspoon whole cloves
- 1 teaspoon red pepper flakes
- 3-inch sprig fresh rosemary
- ½ lemon, sliced
- 1 ½ cup (360 ml) apple cider vinegar
- ½ cup (120 ml) raw honey

Sterilize a 12-ounce (360-ml) mason jar as well as its lid. Lightly pound spices in a mortar and pestle, then add to the jar with the herbs, onion, garlic, and lemon. Fill the jar with the vinegar, cover, and give it a few shakes. Let steep for 2 weeks, shaking every couple of days. Strain, then stir in the honey. Store in the fridge for up to a year.

Note: Use Fire Cider to make Witch's Brew, (page 247) to reap both health and magical benefits.

Magical Correspondences

Use this guide to invoke energies and infuse your recipes, plates, and pairings with intention. While the following correspondences reflect the traditional associations with these ingredients, please note that nothing is universal. For example, if you have a specific emotional connection to a food that clashes with what I've included, then let your personal experience override. Every spell is a personal expression, and that's what makes them all the more powerful.

FOODS, HERBS, SPICES & CELESTIAL BODIES

allspice: money, luck, healing

almond: money, healing, beauty, fertility

apple: love, beauty, luck, divination, known as the food of the dead

apricot: love, peace

asparagus: fertility, male sexuality, expansion

avocado: love, lust, luck, beauty, fertility

barley: love, healing, strength, protection

basil: wealth, love, protection, exorcism

bay: abundance, fortune, success, manifestation, protection, cleansing, healing, psychic powers, prophetic dreams

bean: luck, wealth, prosperity, sex

beet: love, beauty, joy, substitute for blood in spells

blackberry: love, protection

black pepper: protection, purification, quickening, courage, assists with confrontation

blueberry: protection, tranquility, peace, beauty, healing, sleep

buckwheat: abundance, wealth

cabbage: fertility, luck, love

calendula: protection, legal matters, psychic powers

caper: fertility, lust, love

caraway: protection, especially from theft; memory; health; passion; love

cardamom: lust, love

cashew: money

cayenne: protection, quickening, passion, cleansing, repelling negativity especially in relationships

celery: mental powers, lust, male sexuality

chamomile: tranquility, healing, luck

cheese: divination, transformation

cherry: love, fertility, happiness

chili: protection, sexuality, fidelity, hex breaking, quickening, lust, healing, will amplify any intention

chives: protection, focus

chocolate: love, happiness, offerings, spiritual awakening

cilantro: protection, fertility

cinnamon: quickening, expansion, success, healing, strength, love, luck, spirituality

clockwise: calling something in or casting a circle

clove: protection, exorcism, money, healing, psychic power

coffee: dispels nightmares, removes blockages

coriander: love, health, protection

corn: prosperity, fertility, life, protection

counterclockwise: for banishing or reopening a circle

cranberry: love, self-confidence, courage, enthusiasm

cucumber: fertility, healing, tranquility

cumin: protection, especially against theft; fidelity

date: expansion, prosperity

dill: prosperity, protection, luck, lust, confidence, emotional and mental balance

eggplant: abundance, fertility, divination

eggs: fertility, new beginnings, creativity

fennel: strength, protection, cleansing

fig: divination, fertility, love

flaxseed: abundance, wealth, healing

garlic: protection healing, warding off the evil eye, exorcism, quickening

ginger: adventure, new experiences, confidence, success, prosperity, sex, quickening, healing, communication

grapefruit: cleansing, new opportunities, mental clarity

grape: money, fertility, lucid dreaming

hazelnut: protection, wisdom

honey: attraction, love, beauty

horseradish: purification, protection

jasmine: attraction, money, tranquility

lavender: tranquility, sleep, love, protection, communication, offering

leek: love, protection, exorcism

lemon: cleansing, purification, removal of blockages

lettuce: divination, love, peace, money

lime: purification, protection, joy

mango: sensuality, love, fertility, divination

maple: love, money, wealth, luck

marigold: offering, purification, protection

melon: fertility, purification

milk: prosperity, fertility

mint: abundance, communication

mushroom: transformation, intuition, psychic powers, courage, protection

mustard: courage, vitality, sex, passion, clearing financial blockages

nutmeg: money, prosperity, success, luck, protection, breaking hexes

nut: prosperity, protection, fertility

oat: luck, fertility, mental powers

olive: peace, money, health, love, beauty

onion: prosperity, protection against bad influences, endurance, clearing, courage

orange blossom: prosperity, harmony, peace, love

orange: abundance, happiness, love

oregano: joy, strength, vitality, luck, love

paprika: quickening, passion

parsley: tranquility, protection, prosperity, luck

pea: money, fertility

peach: fertility, longevity, love, harmony, wisdom

pear: abundance, fertility, love, lust

pecan: wealth, job security

pineapple: hospitality, protection, luck, money

pistachio: breaking love spells

plum: peace, love, healing
pomegranate: wealth, underworld, divination, fertility, prosperity, transformation
poppy seed: fertility, pleasure, love, luck, heightened awareness
potato: grounding, money, luck, healing
radish: protection, lust
raspberry: love, mend a broken heart
rhubarb: masculine sexuality
rice: love, magic, fertility, protection against evil spirits, rain attractant
rose: love, beauty, friendship, peace
rose hip: beauty, healing, luck, attracts benevolent spirits
rosemary: protection, healing, love, purification

rye: love, self-control
sage: purification, grief, wisdom, mental powers, spirituality, health, longevity
salt: earth energy, protection, purification
sesame: wealth, money, passion, lust
squash, summer: money magic, prosperity, earth energy
squash, winter: prosperity, abundance, health
star anise: divination, love, psychic awareness
strawberry: love, optimism, success, fortune
sugar: attraction, love, lust
sun: energy, creativity, joy
sunflower seed: happiness, creativity, energy, power, protection, wisdom, wishes

thyme: love, loyalty, reputation, protection, purification, beauty, luck, optimism, courage, healing
tomato: prosperity, love
turnip: protection, ending relationships
vanilla: love, lust, passion, energy, peace
vinegar: banishing, binding
walnuts: protection, divinity, blessings, wishes
water: life, healing, emotions, reflection
wheat: abundance, wealth, prosperity

CASTING A CIRCLE

Once you've properly cleansed your space, you can cast a circle with either a wand, smoke bundle, or salt to keep unwanted energies out.

SYMBOLS

circle: completion and protection
cross: union of forces, creation, sex
pentacle: wholeness, unity, earth energy
pentagram: protection

six-pointed: the merging of feminine and masculine as well as the symbol of the Jewish faith
triangle: spirituality, movement, direction, with upward symbolizing masculine energy and downward representing feminine energy

THE ELEMENTS

Earth corresponds to winter, true north, grounding, finances, protection, health, and stability. Evoke this energy with crystals, the tarot suite of pentacles, or salt. The astrological earth signs are Taurus, Virgo, and Capricorn.

Air corresponds to spring, true east, communication, divination, intuition, intellect, and travel. Evoke this energy with incantations, smoke, swords, or the tarot suit of swords. The astrological air signs are Gemini, Libra, and Aquarius.

Fire corresponds to summer, true south, confidence, passion, strength, speed, creativity, and clearing. Evoke this energy with candles, blades, or the tarot suit of wands. The astrological fire signs are Aries, Leo, and Sagittarius.

Water corresponds to autumn, true west, emotions, dreams, depth, purification, feminine energy, the womb, and cleansing. Evoke this energy with moon water, the tarot suit of chalices, or cups. The astrological water signs are Cancer, Scorpio, and Pisces.

CALLING THE QUARTERS

Evoke all four elements in order to strengthen your spell or ritual. Use the following invocation or adapt it in order to better suit your spell or objective.

I call upon Earth in the north for protection. Thank you, Earth.
I call upon Air in the east for wisdom. Thank you, Air.
I call upon Fire in the south for strength. Thank you, Fire.
I call upon Water in the west for cleansing. Thank you, Water.

PHASES OF THE MOON

new: rest, renewal, dreaming, and planting seeds
waxing: expansion, taking action, and nurturing growth

full: accomplishment, abundance, releasing, and harvesting
waning: cleansing, adjustments, reflection, banishing, and tilling the soil

eclipses: chaos and transformation (I don't recommend charging crystals or making moon water during this time, unless you are highly experienced)

THE PLANETARY DAYS OF THE WEEK

The Roman calendar named the days of the week after celestial bodies. Use this correspondence to inform both your spellwork and overall schedule.

Monday: the moon, creativity, divination, intuition, home, family, fertility

Tuesday: Mars, action, passion, strength, vitality, masculinity, sex

Wednesday: Mercury, communication, commerce, intellect, quick trips

Thursday: Jupiter, luck, wealth, expansion, long-distance travel

Friday: Venus, love, friendship, beauty, femininity

Saturday: Saturn, boundaries, responsibility, protection, structure, stability

Sunday: the sun, health, creativity, public image, confidence, strength

COLORS AND NUMBERS

red: passion, sex, courage

pink: love, friendship, beauty, affection, self-love

orange: creativity, confidence, success, generosity

yellow: happiness, communication, optimism, joy

green: wealth, health, fertility, growth, abundance

blue: peace, clarity, insight, imagination

purple: spirituality, divine power, wisdom

white: purity, clarity, light

black: protection, banishing, density, shadow work

brown: grounding, stability, composting

gold: sun, masculine, radiance, prosperity

silver: moon, feminine, intuition

1: individuality, beginnings, focus

2: duality, union, partnership

3: expression, creativity, manifestation

4: stability, structure, balance

5: change, challenge, movement

6: community, union of earth and divine

7: spiritual growth, inner world

8: material growth, wealth, infinity, career

9: completion, fulfillment

KITCHEN TOOLS

wooden spoons: wands and fire or air energy

knives: swords and air or fire energy

pots and pans: cauldrons and water energy

salt: pentacles and earth energy

Mac-and-Cheese
Frittatta, page 51

Index

DEDICATION

This book is dedicated to the memory of my cat Chandler Bing, my familiar, sous chef, and muse. I love you to the moon and back. Thank you for choosing me.

Acknowledgments

I want to start by thanking the team at Indelible Editions. To Dinah for always having my back and working wonders behind the curtain, and to Jen for breathing life into my words with your designing powers. Thank you both for placing your confidence in me.

Thank you to Running Press for the opportunity to create the grimoire of my dreams. To Sara Puppala, and my editors Sara Bader and Randall Lotowycz, for your collaboration and attention to detail. To Devin Forst for your beautiful illustrations. I'm so grateful for your work on *Cheese Magic*.

To my magical mentors at Malliway Brothers and Sideshow Gallery in Chicago. Thank you for helping me improve my craft.

Thank you to my cheese family for all your support and encouragement. To Randall and all my friends at Beautiful Rind, thank you for helping me source the most photogenic cheeses. You are my favorite chapel of Cheesus and Chicago is so lucky to have you.

Thank you to my friends, especially Adrienne, Danielle, and Caroline, for your encouragement and inspiration through the waxes and wanes of my creativity.

Thank you to my mom for your dedication to recipe development and for teaching me the magic in cooking for loved ones. I don't know if I could do this without you. Thank you to my dad for your words of wisdom. Thank you to my entire family and all the ancestors who came before us.

Thank you to Jacob, for tasting my recipes, and constantly supporting me, especially when I doubted myself. I love you so, so much.

Thank you to Hekate, mother of witches, for guiding me as I created my first book on witchcraft.

ABOUT THE AUTHOR

Erika Kubick is a practicing witch and the high priestess behind Cheese Sex Death, a website and social media presence with a mission to educate and excite cheese lovers everywhere. *Cheese Magic* is her second book.